# Reproductive Justice and Women's Voices

# Reproductive Justice and Women's Voices

## *Health Communication across the Lifespan*

Beth Sundstrom

LEXINGTON BOOKS
Lanham • Boulder • New York • London

Published by Lexington Books
An imprint of The Rowman & Littlefield Publishing Group, Inc.
4501 Forbes Boulevard, Suite 200, Lanham, Maryland 20706
www.rowman.com

Unit A, Whitacre Mews, 26-34 Stannary Street, London SE11 4AB



British Library Cataloguing in Publication Information Available

**Library of Congress Cataloging-in-Publication Data**

Sundstrom, Beth L., 1983- , author.
Reproductive justice and women's voices : health communication across the lifespan / Beth L. Sundstrom.
p. cm.
Includes bibliographical references and index.
ISBN 978-1-4985-0313-6 (cloth : alk. paper) -- ISBN 978-1-4985-0314-3 (electronic)
I. Title.
[DNLM: 1. Reproductive Health--United States. 2. Women's Health--United States. 3. Health Communication--United States. 4. Mother-Child Relations--United States. 5. Reproductive Rights--legislation & jurisprudence--United States. 6. Women's Rights--United States. WQ 200 AA1]
RG106.3
362.1981--dc23

2015028195

∞™ The paper used in this publication meets the minimum requirements of American National Standard for Information Sciences Permanence of Paper for Printed Library Materials, ANSI/NISO Z39.48-1992.

Printed in the United States of America

To Bryan, for listening.

# Contents

# Acknowledgments

First and foremost, I would like to thank the women who agreed to participate in this study through interviews. I am grateful for their generous contribution of time, energy, stories, and especially their voices.

I am indebted to the community of scholars and women's health activists in South Carolina. In particular, my colleagues at the College of Charleston, the Medical University of South Carolina (MUSC), and the University of South Carolina provided insightful advice and unwavering support for this project. Serving as co-director of the Women's Health Research Team provided a source of tireless enthusiasm for this work. Thank you to Andrea DeMaria and Merissa Ferrara for your sustaining friendships. Special thanks to research assistants Annalise Baker-Whitcomb and Stephanie Meier for your assistance. Warm thanks to Cynthia Lowenthal for encouraging me to write this book and for providing invaluable guidance since the start of my academic career.

At the University of Maryland, College Park, Robert Gold, Brooke Liu, Kristy Maddux, Elizabeth Toth, and Andrew Wolvin provided critical insight to this project and pushed me to improve the rigor of the research. I am especially grateful to Linda Aldoory for helping me to "unlearn" and for giving me the words to think about health communication and feminist methods. I am inspired by the encouragement and friendship of exceptional communication scholars: Lucinda Austin, Rowena Briones, Mara Hobler, Melissa Janoske, Abbey Levenshus, and Jennifer Vardeman-Winter.

I am indebted to my mentor in public health, Patrick Vivier, for supporting me and this project. Thank you for believing in this idea and the importance of this work. I would like to thank my colleagues and friends at Brown University for their advice and encouragement, especially Priya Hirway, Joann Barao, Lynne Dansereau, and Diane Schlacter. I owe a special debt to the nurses, staff, and the Division of Research at Women & Infants Hospital, especially Susan Swanson-Kubaska. Many thanks to Maureen Phipps for her support and guidance. I acknowledge the generosity of the Brown University Healthy Communities Initiative and the College of Charleston for providing financial support for this research.

Thank you to my editor, Alison Pavan, and the entire team at Rowman & Littlefield and Lexington Books for the privilege of sharing these women's voices with a wider audience. I would also like to thank the anonymous reviewers whose comments improved the precision of the manuscript.

Finally, thank you to my friends, family, and especially my parents, Roberta and Gary Sundstrom. I owe a special debt of gratitude to my husband, Bryan Joffe, for his love and support.

# Introduction and Foundation[1]

The 2010 United States Patient Protection and Affordable Care Act (ACA) addressed gender inequity in health insurance coverage and prompted national debate about women's health decisions. The national health care reform law prevents health insurers from denying coverage or charging higher premiums based on gender or health status (Rangel 2010). Feminist science scholars Wyer et al. (2014) suggest that "the increasing visibility of women's health care in public policy discussions" indicates significant change and progress in women's health (xiv). Between October 1, 2013, and March 31, 2014, more than 4.3 million women enrolled in coverage through the Health Insurance Marketplace established by the ACA (Department of Health and Human Services 2014).

Almost 50 million women with private health insurance benefit from covered women's health preventive services, including breastfeeding support, cancer screening, flu shots, prenatal and maternity care, and all contraception methods approved by the Food and Drug Administration (FDA) (Health Resources and Services Administration 2014). Despite the guarantee of these benefits, a number of recent studies found widespread violations of these rules by health insurers (Sobel, Salganicoff, and Kurani 2015; Benyo, Borchelt, Davenport, Garcia, et al. 2015; Benyo, Borchelt, Davenport, Garrett, et al. 2015). Research suggests that many insurers failed to cover all FDA-approved contraceptive options without cost sharing, especially intrauterine devices (IUDs), hormonal patches, and vaginal rings (Sobel, Salganicoff, and Kurani 2015; Benyo, Borchelt, Davenport, Garrett, et al. 2015).

Although the Supreme Court ruled in favor of the constitutionality of the Affordable Care Act, states and legislators continue to challenge the law, especially in the area of women's reproductive health. In February 2015, the U.S. House of Representatives voted for the 56th time since 2011 on a bill to repeal the Affordable Care Act (Pear 2015). With a failed legislative strategy, opponents of the ACA implemented a series of ongoing lawsuits in court. In 2014, the Supreme Court in *Burwell v. Hobby Lobby* applied the Religious Freedom Restoration Act (RFRA) of 1993 to corporations, ruling that closely held corporations with religious objections are not required to provide coverage of contraception in employer-sponsored health plans (Schwartz 2014). In response to this ruling, sixteen state legislatures introduced state versions of the RFRA with potential to sanction discrimination against lesbian, gay, bisexual, and transgender (LGBT) individuals, as well as significant consequences for reproductive health and contraceptive coverage (Guttmacher Institute 2015). In the first three months of 2015, state legislatures introduced 332 bills to limit women's reproductive health care, including access to abortion (Guttmacher Institute 2015). This fervent opposition to reproductive rights and violations of the Affordable Care Act illustrate the need to investigate women's experiences in this transformative sociopolitical moment.

This book offers an in-depth analysis of women's reproductive health in a political climate redefining women's access to health care. Women's health remains a top public health priority because the health of women and children serves as a proxy for societal health and wellness. The *Healthy People 2020* guidelines champion reducing disparities in maternal and child health as a critical public health goal for the United States. According to Roberts (1997), reproductive liberty must include "the full range of procreative activities, including the ability to bear a child, and it must acknowledge that we make reproductive decisions within a social context, including inequalities of wealth and power" (6). This book contributes to recent efforts to develop a "life course" perspective to address women's health and builds a growing corpus of patient-centered public health literature by analyzing women's reproductive health across the lifespan. Martin (2001) conducted a cultural analysis of reproduction exploring the ways that a diverse group of American women understand and make meaning of reproductive health (such as menstruation, childbirth, and menopause) in the context of culture and the biomedical model. Ultimately, this book investigates how women interpret complicated information about harms and benefits in order to make decisions about their health.

Through an analysis of 81 in-depth interviews conducted between 2010 and 2012 with women ages 18 to 40, this study examines women's reproductive health. According to Haraway (2004), "sex, sexuality, and reproduction are central actors in high-tech myth systems structuring our imaginations of personal and social possibility" (29). This book investigates four critical body episodes: contraceptive use dynamics, pregnancy, childbirth, and the post-partum period. These body episodes explicate women's understandings of control and embodiment in the context of technology and materiality (Warren and Brewis 2004). From a practical perspective, women make complex decisions during these body episodes that offer opportunities for empowerment. Although related areas of reproductive health, such as menstruation and infertility, emerge in the analysis of these episodes, other important areas of women's reproductive health are necessarily omitted. Women's meaning making of each body episode is interrogated in three areas: (1) the physiological experience of reproductive health, (2) perceptions of medicine and the biomedical model, and (3) perceptions of mediated messages about reproduction, including new media.

This chapter explores how health and risk communication has been defined and studied, including the social and political implications of women's reproductive health. First, I outline the biomedical paradigm and the ways that medical understanding of women's health changed based on development of social norms, new screening and diagnostic tools, and improvements in treatment. Then, the historical basis for describing the "ontological" foundation of disease as existing in a Platonic sense independently from the person who experiences the disease is explored (Babrow and Mattson 2008). The challenge of isolating health from attitudes, beliefs, and social values is identified and the alternative biopsychosocial paradigm, which offers a social constructionist approach to illness, health, and medical care, is investigated (Kline 2008). Finally, the methodological approach of the study is detailed and a plan for the book is outlined.

## A POSTMODERN APPROACH

This book takes a postmodern approach to women's health by exploring the woman in the body. According to Babrow and Mattson (2011), "health communication is significant for the pronounced and profound tensions and interplay between the realms of communication and the body" (19). The body's centrality to the physical process and cultural understandings of reproduction requires investigation of the body as a core feature of analysis. In the tradition of feminist science studies, I am concerned with, "critiquing distortions and misrepresentations of women's minds and bodies in medical and scientific research and development (i.e., documenting and demonstrating the social construction of knowledge) [and] . . . exploring technoscientific innovations as both colluding and colliding with the sex/gender/sexuality nexus" (Wyer et al. 2014, xxi).

This study builds on theoretical work examining power, control, and hegemony as regulatory controls of the body and reproduction (Foucault 1978). Gramsci's theories of hegemony, which he developed in the 1920s and 1930s, suggest that individuals' common sense understandings often reinforce oppressive dominant ideologies (Gramsci 1971). According to van Zoonen (1994), "dominant ideology becomes invisible because it is translated into 'common sense,' appearing as the natural, unpolitical state of things accepted by each and everyone" (24). This analysis responds to the call of feminist science scholars to "strive for more livable worlds beyond the hegemonic tales of progress, of technoscience as biological, and technological determination means also to reinterpret what counts as nature, as sex, or as gender" (Weber 2014, 551). As Simone de Beauvoir argues in *The Second Sex*, "one is not born, but rather becomes, woman" (2011, 283).

This book interrogates women's reproductive health across the lifespan. Foucault (1978) argues that biopolitics led to the "hysterization of women's bodies," which medicalized reproduction and relegated natural processes to the biomedical paradigm. In a postmodern context, women's bodies serve as a site through which personal and social identity is formed in relation to gender and reproduction. Health communication scholar Cline (2011)

> calls for researchers to understand health and risk behaviors in terms of the frames of meaning used in the interpersonal contexts in which the behavior occurs. More specifically, we can begin this shift in perspective by investigating the identity and relational meanings associated with health-and risk-behaviors. In turn, we can build interventions on these messages and meanings. (394)

This focus on identity reflects the worldview that individuals make sense of everyday life by (re)constructing social realities (van Zoonen 1994). From a health communication perspective, "the communicative interweaving of bodily sensation, cognitive-emotional sense-making, and various layers of social structures and practices fabricate the social meaning of physical states and the physical meaning of social states" (Babrow and Mattson 2011, 19).

Social expectations regarding reproduction define and limit women's gendered role in society, often dictating women's understanding of their bodies. According to Butler (2010),

> the critical task is, rather, to locate strategies of subversive repetition enabled by those constructions, to affirm the local possibilities of intervention through participating in precisely those practices of repetition that constitute identity and, therefore, present the immanent possibility of contesting them. (201)

This study extends understandings of medicalization, defined as the pathologizing of women's bodies, which marginalizes women and triggers an identity struggle (Pollock 1999; Martin 2001).

The existing research and analysis of gender, reproduction, and the body substantiates the need for further inquiry into the social constructs that contribute to the understanding of women's health. According to Martin (2001), "although we tend to think of science as outside culture because it seeks the truth about nature, I assert that it is in fact more like a hegemonic system"

(22). Science emerges as a cultural practice regulated by values, language, and politics of representation (Weber 2014). Bird and Rieker (2008) address the ways that gender interacts with governments, communities, families, and individuals to influence personal health. This book elaborates the social constructionist approach, which views health and illness as constructed by preexisting meanings, values, beliefs, experiences, and shared cultural understandings.

This study examines representations of the biomedical paradigm, the traditional view of health and illness through which the medical establishment locates disease in the body, identified and defined by objective signs and symptoms. According to Kline (2011), the professionalization of the medical establishment established its power over illness and health through the medicalization of the body. This perspective does not negate the possibility of empowerment through technology in women's health. This book builds on Donna Haraway's cyborg feminist perspective, which suggests that "disrupting the nature/culture duality will not only free us from the constraints of essentialism but will also allow us to conceive of and employ science and technology to further women's aims in a more nuanced manner" (Aengst and Layne 2014, 184). By talking with women, this study privileges the voices of individual women and allows their stories and understandings to emerge.

Finally, this book contributes to a culture-centered approach to public health research and practice, which is paramount in developing effective health communication campaigns. According to Dutta and Basu (2011), "the culture-centered approach argues that the undermining of the agency of subaltern groups is quintessential to the erasures of these groups from the dominant epistemic structures, from policy platforms, and from spaces of campaign design and development" (329). In this view, revealing the voices and health experiences of marginalized populations offers opportunities to address inequity and implement social change (Dutta and Basu 2011).

This study employs a feminist research perspective, which acknowledges that sex, race, and class intersect in complicated ways (Berger and Guidroz 2010; hooks 1984). Although there has been some progress in the reproductive justice movement in recent years to address these intersections, Roberts (1997) argued that "the feminist focus on gender and identification of male domination as the source of reproductive repression often overlooks the importance of racism in shaping our understanding of reproductive liberty and the degree of 'choice' that women really have" (5). According to bell hooks (1984), "there is much evidence substantiating the reality that race and class identity creates differences in quality of life, social status, and lifestyle that take precedence over the common experience women share—differences which are rarely transcended" (4). Smith (1988) also addresses the struggle of difference and the challenge of intersectionality "in political struggles, there wouldn't be any 'your' and 'my' issues, if we saw each form of oppression as integrally linked to the others" (77). This analysis attempts to acknowledge the body as a potential site of racist and sexist ideologies (Minh-ha 1989).

Numerous campaigns seek to persuade women regarding health and policy issues, ranging from preconception care to home births. Ehrenreich and English (2005) expose and challenge the pseudo-science that impacts women's lives surrounding menstruation and pregnancy. As health and policy campaigns target women, it is essential for campaign planners and legislators to understand this audience. Cline (2011) warns:

> In the name of "doing good," that is, acting with moral certitude, many in the fields of medicine, public health, and health communication risk doing harm. When public health officials design and disseminate messages for the public with more consideration for their political and moral acceptability than how those messages will be interpreted and practiced with the social realities in which various targeted publics live, they risk doing more harm than good. (394)

This study provides a lens to explore women's perceptions and use of new media, mass media, and interpersonal communication channels. In particular, this book addresses how advances in medical technology and new media have impacted women's perceptions of reproduction and health. Public health practitioners, health care providers, and campaign planners will benefit from improved understandings of women's identity, perceptions, and opportunities for empowerment and agency around reproductive health.

## PATIENT-CENTERED PUBLIC HEALTH

Public health is an interdisciplinary field focused on promoting health and preventing disease in a community or population. Major achievements credited to public health in the twentieth century include vaccinations and the control of infectious diseases, safer foods and fluoridation of drinking water, motor-vehicle and occupational safety, family planning and contraceptive access, and smoking cessation. These public health improvements increased life expectancy by twenty-five years, while improvements in medicine added only five years to the average life span of an American citizen (Centers for Disease Control and Prevention 1999). According to Parrott and Kreuter (2011), health communication is linked to "a wide range of long-standing disciplines like public health, health promotion, health education, and patient education, as well as more recent and emerging disciplines like social marketing, medical decision making, and e-health" (5).

In order to promote health and prevent illness and disability, public health practitioners investigate the natural history of disease through the study of epidemiology (Schneider 2010). Health communication scholars transcend disciplinary boundaries by integrating epidemiology and social sciences to develop innovative solutions to public health problems (Parrott and Kreuter 2011). Health communication operates at the fundamental core of human experience, connecting health and illness through the body, mind, and society (Babrow and Mattson 2008). Health communication is defined as a matrix of formal and informal messages, in which intended and spontaneous everyday messages abound, in both mediated and interpersonal contexts (Cline 2008). Patient-centered public health emphasizes the importance of mutual trust and control in the patient-provider relationship and decision making process. In this approach, the physician serves as health advisor and offers information from a variety of sources, which empowers the patient to ask questions.

## RISK COMMUNICATION

Patient-centered public health involves communicating about risk. According to Turner, Skubisz, and Rimal (2011),

> effective risk communication is vital to individuals' health. People weigh the pros and cons of medications, treatments, and prevention and detection options so that they can live longer and healthier lives. Risk communicators must relay risks and benefits of these health decisions effectively so that individuals can make sound decisions. As such, risk communication is not about telling people what to do, but it is about providing people with information aimed at helping them make informed decisions. (147)

Health communication is critical in women's understandings of (dis)ease and risk in relation to screening. According to Aschengrau and Seague (2008), screening identifies individuals with abnormalities who do not yet show signs or symptoms of disease. The practice of screening assumes that diseases progress linearly and if detected early will result in earlier and improved treatment and survival (Aschengrau and Seague 2008). The World Health Organization (2007) identifies a number of requisite conditions for a disease to be suitable for screening. Specifically, the disease must represent an important health problem worth the cost and effort of screening. The disease must be detectable during a lengthy preclinical phase in the natural history of the disease. Abnormalities in the asymptomatic phase that will progress to clinical lesions must be significant. There must be an acceptable treatment available that depends on earlier diagnosis to lengthen a patient's life. Finally, the screening test must be acceptable to patients and available at a reasonable cost (WHO 2007).

## *Evaluating Screening*

The recommendation for whether or not a screening test should be used in a certain population is based on the validity of the test. In other words, validity is the ability of the test to accurately identify the existence of preclinical disease. In screening tests, validity is measured by sensitivity and specificity. Sensitivity is the effectiveness of a screening test in detecting disease among those who have it. Specificity is the likelihood that the test will provide negative results among those who are free of disease (Gordis 2008). Many screening tests favor sensitivity over specificity, increasing the probability that the test will yield more false positives than false negatives (Schneider 2010). In this approach, the test will almost always correctly identify individuals with preclinical disease, however, many individuals without the disease will also be falsely identified.

Individuals who receive a positive screening test are typically referred for more specific diagnostic tests. These tests can be more invasive and more expensive than the original screening protocol. As a result, the true costs of screening must include the adverse effects experienced by patients. Patients report anxiety, pain, psychological distress, and adverse outcomes associated with diagnostic follow-up procedures. Experts cite increased radiation exposure, unnecessary tests and treatment, as well as increased health care costs related to the adverse effects of screening on women.

While the true costs of screening are often minimized, the benefits of screening are overestimated. Evaluations of screening programs often exhibit lead-time bias, volunteer bias, length-bias sampling, and overdiagnosis bias. Lead-time bias examines the survival rate of individuals who were screened compared to those who were diagnosed without screening. Lead-time bias overestimates the benefit of screening because "survival may appear longer among screened individuals simply because their diagnoses were made earlier, not because they actually lived longer" (Gordis 2008, 418). Furthermore, since screening often leads to additional tests and surgeries, the treatments following diagnosis may actually lead to the earlier death of screened patients (Schneider 2010). Volunteer bias suggests that those who volunteer for screening may be different in important ways compared to those who do not engage in screening. Length-bias sampling and overdiagnosis bias indicate that abnormalities identified through screening may never cause symptoms or be life-threatening (Schneider 2010).

## *Evolution of Screening Recommendations*

The evolution of screening recommendations can be traced to the development of intuitive thought within the medical community and the American Medical Association (AMA), as well as the cultural emphasis on uncertainty reduction. Croswell, Ransohoff, and Kramer (2010) offer an extensive history of the principles of cancer screening. They argue that intuitive reasoning and the reliance on personal observations led to the science of early detection in cancer control, which dominated medical practice during the late nineteenth and twentieth centuries. According to Croswell, Ransohoff, and Kramer (2010), the American Medical Association endorsed the periodic health exam for early disease detection in the 1920s, reinforcing the linear model of disease development that became the basis for cancer screening. It wasn't until the 1960s that researchers began conducting randomized, controlled clinical trials to evaluate the effectiveness of screening programs (Aschengrau and Seague 2008).

An evidence-based approach remains "inconsistently applied to early detection programs, policies, and belief systems in the United States" (Croswell, Ransohoff, and Kramer 2010, 215). According to Babrow and Kline (2000), despite mixed research findings on the effectiveness of breast self-exams (BSE), there is a one-sided media and biomedical discourse in the United States that assumes the procedure will detect cancer early, thereby reducing the threat of cancer and the uncertainty associated with the disease. The authors argue that the ideology of uncertainty reduction as a foundation for BSE may disempower women and pose a threat to their health (Babrow and Kline 2000).

The history of intuitive thinking and personal observation continues to impact assumptions about the effectiveness of screening in the United States. However, an evidence-based approach to screening recommendations is beginning to address biases inherent in early disease detection, such as lead-time bias, volunteer bias, length-bias sampling, and overdiagnosis bias. According to Welch, Schwartz, and Woloshin (2012),

> we are in a midst of a paradigm shift in how we think about cancer. Our efforts to find cancer early with screening tests has shown that what pathologists call cancer encompasses a set of cellular abnormalities with very heterogeneous growth rates that vary from very fast to completely static. That's right, some cancers don't progress at all. Some cancers will never make a difference to patients. The idea that some cancers don't matter is a radical one for the medical field. (53)

The U.S. Preventive Services Task Force (USPSTF or Task Force) offers one evidence-based approach to weighing the potential harms and benefits of screening programs. The USPSTF was created in 1984 as an independent group of 16 national experts in prevention and evidence-based medicine, most are practicing clinicians, who volunteer their time to improve the health of Americans by making evidence-based recommendations about clinical preventive services, such as screenings (AHRQ 2013). The USPSTF conducts scientific evidence reviews and develops recommendations for clinicians and health systems. For the USPSTF to make a recommendation, the benefits must outweigh the harms. The Task Force focuses on maintenance of health and quality of life as the major benefits of clinical preventive services, and not simply the identification of disease. USPSTF recommendations form the basis of the clinical standards for many professional societies, health organizations, and medical quality review groups (USPSTF Program Office 2013).

### *Screening in Women's Health*

Examples of screening tests in women's health include breast-self exams and mammograms to detect breast cancer, Pap tests to identify cervical cancer, and tests for markers of ovarian cancer.

### *Breast Cancer*

In November 2009, the USPSTF released new guidelines for breast cancer screening. These recommendations updated the September 2002 guidelines, which recommended screening mammography with or without clinical breast exam every one to two years for women aged 40 and older. In 2009, the Task Force recommended against routine screening mammography in women aged 40 to 49 years. Instead, biennial screening mammography is recommended for women between the ages of 50 and 74 years. The USPSTF concluded that the current evidence is insufficient to assess the additional benefits and harms of clinical breast examination beyond screening mammography in women 40 years or older. However, the Task Force recommended against clinicians teaching women how to perform breast self-examination. This recommendation reinforces Babrow and Kline's (2000) finding that breast self-exam may disempower women.

The USPSTF found that 1,904 women aged 39 to 49 needed to be invited for annual screening for ten years to prevent one breast cancer death (leaving 1,903 women at substantial risk of overdiagnosis) (Baines 2011). According to Croswell, Ransohoff, and Kramer (2010), U.S. SEER data over a period of thirty years indicate that increases in the total breast cancer rate result from increases in early-stage disease, with little difference in the incidence of late-stage disease. This represents overdiagnosis bias, which occurs when more early-stage cases of disease are identified than late-stage cases of disease prevented.

### *Cervical Cancer*

Recent recommendations regarding cervical cancer screening aim to lessen harms, which include "direct complications from screening and confirmatory tests; the expense, anxiety, and life disruptions incurred with new diagnoses with unclear clinical significance; and the prolonged surveillance endured by patients with positive tests but no evidence of disease" (Sawaya 2009, 2503). In November 2009, the American College of Obstetricians and Gynecologists (ACOG) issued new guidelines for cervical cancer screening that increase the age of screening initiation to 21, increase screening intervals to every two years, and discontinue screening between ages 65 and 70.

The USPSTF corroborated these changes with slight adjustments in 2012, recommending screening for cervical cancer among women aged 21 to 65 years every three years or for women aged 30 to 65 years who want to lengthen the screening interval to every five years with HPV co-testing (Moyer 2012a). ACOG and the USPSTF recommend against screening for cervical cancer in women younger than age 21 years because cytologic abnormalities are common among this age group and may result in a variety of harms, including extended surveillance and invasive procedures (Sawaya 2009). The new guidelines caution against treatment, such as cervical cryotherapy or electrosurgical loop excision, among young women, because these procedures can result in negative consequences for a woman's future fertility and pregnancies (Croswell, Ransohoff, and Kramer 2010). According to Sawaya (2009), these recommendations minimize harm by advocating less screening among low-risk women, including younger women.

### *Ovarian Cancer*

Although protein biomarkers can be identified for early detection of ovarian cancer, no professional associations recommend screening for ovarian cancer at this time (Nolen and Lokshin 2012). The USPSTF continues to recommend against screening for ovarian cancer in women citing the high frequency of false-positive results that lead to unnecessary procedures with high complication rates, which ultimately do not reduce death rates (Moyer 2012b).

### *Media Representations of Screening*

Health communication campaigns aimed at cancer screening began in the 1930s in the United States. In 1936, the American Cancer Society, then known as the American Society for the Control of Cancer, developed a national communication campaign, "the Women's Field Army," to "wage war" on cancer. The campaign raised money and educated the public about cancer and the importance of screening (ACS 2012). According to Croswell, Ransohoff, and Kramer (2010), "'Delay Kills!' was a frequent slogan; one poster released during WWII claimed that more people died every 2 weeks from a delayed cancer diagnosis than had died at Pearl Harbor" (203–204). A 1970s American Cancer Society campaign poster read, "If you're a woman over 35, be sure to schedule a mammogram. Unless you're still not convinced of its importance. In which case, you may need more than your breasts examined. Find the time. Have a mammogram. Give yourself the chance of a lifetime" (Woloshin et al. 2012). More recently, Memorial Sloan-Kettering Cancer Center ran an ad in the *New York Times Magazine*: "The early warning signs of colon cancer: You feel great. You have a healthy appetite. You're only 50" (Woloshin et al. 2012).

Women are also exposed to media representations of screening through news coverage. According to Jensen et al. (2011), news coverage of cancer research "rarely contains discourse-based hedging, including caveats, limitations, and uncertainties" (486). Through a multiple message experiment, the authors found that news consumers understand and support scientific uncertainty and discourse-based hedging in cancer news coverage (Jensen et al. 2011). The news coverage of the November 2009 USPSTF recommendations for breast cancer screening followed this pattern by simplifying the content of the recommendations (Plutynski 2012).

The November 2009 USPSTF revised recommendations for breast cancer screening resulted in a national controversy, which played out in the news media. While the guidelines remained front-page news for several consecutive days, common themes emerged regarding the threat of rationing health care, the impact on advocacy organizations, such as the American Cancer Society, and personal stories of women who had breast cancer diagnosed in their forties (Truog 2009). A content analysis of news stories during the controversy found that the majority of articles and social media posts (51.9%) did not support the new screening recommendations, with only 17.6% supporting the change (Squiers et al. 2011).

In an analysis of newspaper coverage of the benefits and harms of mammography, Holmes-Rovner and Charles (2003) found that articles manufactured polarization of opinion by highlighting the dichotomy between experts and advocates. The authors emphasized the value of discussing uncertainty inherent in medical technologies to improve evidence-based patient choice (Holmes-Royner and Charles 2003). Building on channel complementarity theory and media-system dependency theory, Weeks et al. (2012) found that conflict-oriented news coverage of the new guidelines predicted mammography-related Google searches online.

## *Risk in Women's Cancer Screening*

The risk of false positives and overdiagnosis is a major harm associated with screening programs. A false positive result often leads to anxiety, additional medical appointments, and more invasive diagnostic tests. The benefits of screening in terms of mortality reduction must be weighed against the cumulative risk of false positives and overdiagnosis. Keen and Keen (2009) investigated the likelihood of screening mammography to save women's lives and discovered that of those with screen-detectable cancer, mammography saves less than 5% of women's lives.

According to a meta-analysis of trials including 600,000 women undergoing screening mammography, Gøtzsche and Nielsen (2011) found that for every 2,000 women screened over a ten-year period, only one life will be prolonged, while 10 healthy women will be treated unnecessarily, and more than 200 women will experience a false positive. To put it another way, Hubbard, Miglioretti, and Smith (2010) estimate the risk of a false positive result after ten screening mammograms to be between 58% and 77%.

False positive tests result in real harm to women. Women describe anxiety about cervical cancer screening and an abnormal pap test result causes high levels of distress and clinically meaningful anxiety for up to 12 weeks, which impacts mental health and may lead women to discontinue screening (Cooper 2011; Drolet et al. 2012). According to Hafslund and Nortvedt (2009), the influence of waiting and follow-up visits after a false positive mammography result may negatively impact women's emotional health, well-being, and quality of life for months. Croswell et al. (2009) analyzed the Prostate, Lung, Colorectal, and Ovarian (PLCO) cancer screening trial and found that false-positive ovarian cancer results from transvaginal ultrasounds resulted in major surgeries. In this trial, up to 40% of women with a false-positive result submitted to a laparotomy, hysterectomy, and/or oophorectomy (Croswell, Ransohoff, and Kramer 2010).

Overdiagnosis occurs when abnormalities identified through screening may never cause symptoms or be life-threatening. The developers of early disease detection programs assumed that screening would increase the incidence of early cancer diagnosis, while decreasing the rates of late-stage cancers. U.S. SEER data shows that this assumption was flawed based on the rates of advanced cancer diagnosis. The rate of overdiagnosis in breast cancer screening has been estimated as high as 50% (Hersch et al. 2013). In a population-based study in Norway, Kalager et al. (2012) found that 15% to 25% of breast cancers are overdiagnosed through mammography screening. These estimates represent a substantial amount of overdiagnosis.

According to Baines (2011), the consequences of overdiagnosis may persist over the course of a person's life. The results of unnecessary treatment may include pain, deformity, and increased risk of cardiac complications over the long term (Baines 2011). In a qualitative study, Hersch et al. (2013) found that awareness of breast cancer overdiagnosis among women is limited. These women were surprised to learn about the risk of overdiagnosis and valued information about it. The authors emphasized the importance of communication about overdiagnosis and how rates may influence screening and treatment decisions (Hersch et al. 2013).

## *Communicating Risk*

The field of health communication evolved to spread one-way messages from the scientific community and policy makers to the public. These messages promoted expert-desired health behaviors, such as cancer screening (e.g., Woloshin et al. 2012; Croswell, Ransohoff, and Kramer 2010). The growing need to balance the harms and benefits of health behaviors led health communicators to favor an iterative approach to risk management incorporating perspectives from experts and individuals (Scherer and Juanillo 2008). According to Babrow and Mattson (2011),

> the debate between ontological and holistic models of disease/illness reflects the basic tension between idiosyncrasy and commonality in health communication. This tension constitutes a fault line in scholarly conceptions of health care and promotion, within the interactions of patients and care providers, and in the conceptions of risk as they are understood by health communicators and their audience members. For example, the tension is reflected in the ever-present possibility of debates over relative expertise, what counts as legitimate evidence, the meanings of (relative) risk, decision making, and so on. (22–23)

In a qualitative study of the interplay between lay and professional understandings of cervical cancer risk, Armstrong and Murphy (2008) found that contemporary professional medical explanations of risk proved ineffective. Instead, they advocate a more accessible explanation of cancer causation, which incorporates the context of women's lives and experiences (Armstrong and Murphy 2008).

Women's lived experience and risk perceptions vary by demographic characteristics. According to Haggstrom and Schapira (2006), African American women were more likely than white women to accurately perceive breast cancer risk in terms of survival and the benefit of screening mammography. African American women were more likely to describe a pessimistic perception of the benefit of mammography. The authors suggest that awareness of risk perceptions is critical to improve patient-physician communication (Haggstrom and Schapira 2006). Nekhlyudov and Braddock (2009) develop a patient-centered model dialogue to educate and engage women in understanding potential benefits and harms in order to make an informed decision about initiating screening mammography.

Communication about screening is an essential component of promoting better understanding of risks and benefits. According to Squiers et al. (2011), the 2009 USPSTF mammography recommendations confused women about when they should get a mammogram. The authors identify the importance of strategy and language in releasing future recommendations in order to limit confusion among consumers, providers, and advocacy groups (Squiers et al. 2011). In a clinical setting, the quality of physician communication skills and physicians' communication style influences screening behaviors (Fox et al. 2009; Meguerditchian et al. 2012; Politi et al. 2008). Resistance to improving patient-provider communication strategies around screening may be linked to studies suggesting that providing women with additional information about risks and benefits of screening does not modify participation rates (Giordano et al. 2012). Physicians may also resist engaging with Internet-informed patients if they consider their patients' online information seeking a nuisance for their professional practice because it interrupts the flow of the visit (Caiata-Zuffrey and Schulz 2012).

Women deserve better information about the risks and benefits of screening. Physicians may need more direction in how to discuss complicated risk information and engage women in the decision making process about screening. According to Covey (2011), the quality of an individual's decision making process may be altered by the format used to present treatment benefits. Wegwarth and Gigerenzer (2011) found that a sample of German gynecologists were not able to correctly and transparently communicate the harms and benefits of mammography screening to a patient. While data about screening was rarely mentioned, when these physicians provided numerical information, they often quantified the benefit using relative risk reduction (Wegwarth and Gigerenzer 2011). When physicians and risk communicators discuss early disease detection in terms of relative risk reduction, they tend to overstate the benefits of screening.

According to Jensen and Trussell (2012), media outlets tend to report relative measures of risk and rarely present information about absolute risk. Great Britain's National Health Service presented relative risk as opposed to absolute risk reductions in pamphlets about screening (Thornton, Edwards, and Baum 2003). Absolute risk rather than relative risk is the most accurate way to discuss screening and to support consumer-oriented informed medical decision making (Keen and Keen 2009). Covey (2011) found that "presenting baseline risks using natural frequencies may help to reduce the biasing effects of relative risks" (788). Hanoch (2004) mirrors this recommendation, suggesting that natural frequencies offer an improved approach for physicians and patients to discuss complicated probabilities and statistical information related to the potential risks and benefits of screening and treatment.

The history of intuitive thinking, personal observation, and the ideology of uncertainty reduction continues to impact assumptions about women's health, including the effectiveness of screening programs. Experts have begun to question the benefits of screening programs, particularly among younger women. Data suggests that screening programs have not fulfilled their promise in lowering mortality rates. As a result, there is a growing need for physicians and health communicators to provide a more balanced discussion of the harms and benefits of screening and treatment, which acknowledges women's lived experiences.

## A FEMINIST APPROACH

This book employs a feminist research perspective, which acknowledges the fundamental inequality of women and strives to create social change. According to Hesse-Biber, Nagy, and Leavy (2007),

> by documenting women's lives, experiences, and concerns, illuminating gender-based stereotypes and biases, and unearthing women's subjugated knowledge, feminist research challenges the basic structures and ideologies that oppress women. Feminist research goals foster empowerment and emancipation for women and other marginalized groups, and feminist researchers often apply their findings in the service of promoting social change and social justice for women. (4)

Cirksena and Cuklanz (1992) suggest that feminist research ultimately seeks to understand and overcome the subjugation of women.

Feminist scholars are guided by the belief that women's lives, experiences, and point of view or standpoint are important (Harding 2004; Hawkesworth 2006). Feminist researchers provide a window to the personal experiences of women by exploring feelings and experiences in a purposeful way (Smith 2004). In addition to valuing the experience and voices of women, feminist research is influenced by relationships. Feminist research addresses the hierarchy inherent in the researcher-researched relationship (Letherby 2003). According to some feminist researchers, "self-disclosure initiates *true dialogue* by allowing participants to become *co-researchers*" (Reinharz 1992). Other ways that feminist researchers validate relationships include "woman-to-woman" talk, closeness, and reciprocated nurturing.

The goal of feminist research is to help participants understand and change their situations by giving voice to the voiceless. A feminist perspective offers an opportunity to empower women where the researcher serves as a "listener and a participant who engages in dialogue with the members of the community. Dialogue introduces the voices of cultural participants into the discursive space, which has largely omitted them or treated them as absent" (Dutta and Basu 2011, 331). This research study served as an opportunity for women to talk about health issues important to them. Participants described the realization that they feel silenced by their inability to speak about health issues. This research empowered participants by providing a protected time and space for these women to discuss their own health needs and opinions.

## CONVERSATIONS WITH WOMEN

Between 2010 and 2012, I conducted extensive, semi-structured qualitative interviews with 81 women (ages 18 to 40). I endeavored to "deal with the way women relate to dominant cultural categories through the medium of conversations about their bodily processes" (Martin 2001, 22). Eighteen (18) of these women were female college students (ages 18 to 24) enrolled in a large, public university in the Mid-Atlantic region of the United States. I interviewed 19 pregnant women (ages 24 to 38) who lived in an urban area on the East Coast. To recruit college students and pregnant women, I used purposive and snowball sampling techniques through acquaintances, informal contacts, and word of mouth. Theoretical sampling improved maximum variation in terms of a variety of contextual factors. The research protocol and procedures were approved by the appropriate Institutional Review Boards and all participants provided informed consent to participate in the project. In-depth interviews were conducted with participants at sites comfortable for participants, such as coffee shops, office locations, or the participants' homes. I conducted 44 interviews with biological mothers of newborns (ages 18 to 40) in the immediate post-partum period. I recruited women in the maternity ward of a hospital in an urban area on the East Coast. Interviews were conducted at the hospital or over the telephone within two weeks of delivery.

Overall, 22 participants (27%) self-identified as women of color (African American; biracial; Hispanic; Asian; other) and 59 participants self-identified as white (73%). Among participants, 16 participants earned a high school degree or less (20%), 27 reported some college (33%), 23 earned a four-year bachelor's degree (28%), and 15 participants earned a graduate degree (19%). According to the U.S. Census Bureau (2013), approximately 58% of adults 25 and over have attended some college.

## INTERVIEWING

Interviews are essential to understand how individuals make meaning of their daily lives. According to Rubin and Rubin (2012), interviews should be a "conversational partnership," where the interviewer can guide the conversation, while allowing new ideas and pertinent directions to emerge. This method of data collection is particularly relevant to this study as a cultural approach to the medicalization of women's bodies. According to Sharf and Vanderford (2008), interviewing offers the opportunity to join medical discourse with women's everyday experiences in order to create a shared story for the purpose of medical choice and treatment.

Lindlof and Taylor (2010) suggest that qualitative interviews do not depend on the "accuracy" of what participants say; instead, the researcher is interested in how respondents express themselves in the context of the interview. This study employed semi-structured interview protocols, which prepares a list of questions, but allows flexibility for the researcher to change questions during the interview. According to Rubin and Rubin (2012), it makes little sense to ask the same questions to each participant in qualitative research. In other words, remaining open to the natural flow of the conversation allows participants the freedom to discuss topics and issues that are most important to them. I paid particular attention to developing interview guides that would provide opportunities to build rapport with participants, which creates an environment of respect and invites self-expression and permission to talk freely (Lindlof and Taylor 2010).

Analytical techniques from the grounded theory approach provided an inductive method of analysis, which privileges the voices of participants and allows their stories and understandings to emerge (Glaser and Strauss 1967). Corbin and Strauss (2008) suggest that grounded theory reflects the social justice aim of feminism in its attempt to bring about social change through practical research that develops pragmatic knowledge. According to Corbin and Strauss (2008), qualitative analysis is a process of examining and interpreting data in order to find meaning, improve understanding, and develop knowledge. Corbin and Strauss (2008) suggest that grounded theory is no longer limited to theory construction. Instead, researchers may apply the analytic techniques and procedures of grounded theory to develop new knowledge without theory building. Furthermore, Corbin and Strauss (2008) make room for researchers to build on an existing program of research and to employ a theoretical framework, which offers insight, direction, and a foundation of concepts to draw from during analysis. Scholars in health communication have employed a grounded theory methodology to derive constructs and themes from qualitative data to better understand publics and improve campaign design (Tindall and Vardeman-Winter 2011; Vardeman and Aldoory 2008; Vardeman-Winter 2012). Corbin and Strauss (2008) maintain that qualitative analysis is a process that cannot be rigidly codified. As a result, I remained open to new concepts that emerged from the data.

Each audio-recorded interview and memo was either typed or transcribed verbatim and entered into HyperRESEARCH 3.5.2 qualitative analysis software. The use of this computer-assisted analysis software offered a number of benefits for organizing interviews and comparing notes with transcripts. I used HyperRESEARCH to assist with data analysis. A constant-comparative method was conducted throughout data collection to analyze transcripts (Corbin and Strauss 2008). I coded the transcripts line-by-line, comparing each transcript against the next for similarities and differences. This process of coding relies on deriving and developing concepts from data (Berg 2009).

According to Corbin and Strauss (2008), open coding allows the researcher to focus on words and meanings, which aids in breaking down data into concepts. I also conducted axial coding, which relates concepts to each other across data. As the researcher identifies conceptually similar incidents, Corbin and Strauss (2008) recommend using in-vivo codes, which privilege the words of research participants.

I employed the conditional/consequential matrix as an analytic device to stimulate contextual interpretation of data based on the broad range of conditions and consequences that determine context (Corbin and Strauss 2008). I used memos and observer comments during the data collection and analysis process to maintain reflexivity and to identify emerging concepts (Rubin and Rubin 2012). Throughout the data collection process, I compared and analyzed transcripts, observer comments, and memos. I engaged in self-reflexivity through journaling and memoing to improve the empirical rigor of this inquiry. Self-reflexivity ensures construct validity by revealing how the researcher's beliefs and theoretical understandings impact the opportunity for alternative explanations (Lather 1991). I further improved validity by checking for representativeness, triangulating data, checking for outliers and extreme cases, looking for negative evidence, and seeking feedback from participants (Silverman and Marvasti 2008). In addition, I used raw qualitative data in the form of verbatim quotes to define key concepts and themes in order to allow the reader to assess face and content validity of the data (Guest and MacQueen 2008).

## OUTLINE AND STRUCTURE

Chapter 1 explores the integration of body and self in contraceptive use dynamics. Since 1960, American women have been able to prevent pregnancy with the oral contraceptive pill. Despite widespread use of this highly effective form of birth control, half of all pregnancies in the United States remain unplanned. Research indicates that women are increasingly familiar with a variety of contraceptive methods; however, women remain skeptical of pursuing a range of birth control options, and as a result, the contraceptive needs of women continue to be unmet.

College women, ages 18 to 24 years, have the highest rates of unintended pregnancies and induced abortions, which has largely been attributed to lack of contraceptive use. At least 80% of college females are sexually active and at risk of unintended pregnancy. Chapter 1 provides a foundation for understanding female college students' knowledge, perceptions, and use of contraceptive methods. I present 18 in-depth interviews with young women ages 18 to 23 to explore their attitudes and perceptions of contraceptive options. Specifically, this chapter explores women's meaning making of contraception in three areas: (1) the physiological experience of contraception, (2) perceptions of medicine and the biomedical model surrounding contraception, and (3) perceptions of mediated messages about contraception.

Chapter 2 deconstructs issues of identity, power, and body politics by (re)writing the body. This chapter explicates the body politic of pregnancy and offers an understanding of how medicalization has impacted women's experience of pregnancy. This analysis answers the questions: (1) How do women make meaning of the physiological experience of pregnancy?; (2) How do women make meaning of the medical experiences they have encountered during pregnancy?; and (3) How do women make meaning of campaigns and messages addressing pregnancy, from prenatal health to home births?

I present the results of in-depth interviews with 19 pregnant women ages 24 to 38 to understand their perceptions of pregnancy. The women were between 15 and 37 weeks pregnant at the time of the interview. Chapter 2 uncovers pregnant women's body identity, perceptions, and opportunities for empowerment and agency.

Following the discussion of pregnancy and expectations of labor and delivery, chapter 3 describes the experience of childbirth. I present findings from 44 in-depth interviews with biological mothers of newborns in the immediate post-partum period. All interviews were conducted within two weeks of the birth of an infant, many in the hospital maternity ward. Among participants, although each experience was unique, listening to and understanding these women's birth stories created a unique rapport between researcher and participant. This chapter explores (1) the physiological experience of childbirth, (2) perceptions of medicine and the biomedical model surrounding childbirth, and (3) perceptions of mediated messages about childbirth. Participants' birth stories offered an in-depth understanding of their values, their relationship with their doctor, and their beliefs regarding the medical model.

Chapter 4 delves deeper into how the mother-child dyad impacts women's meaning making of health. I present additional results from the same 44 women interviewed during the post-partum period. This chapter addresses (1) the physiological basis of reproductive health and motherhood, (2) perceptions of medicine and the biomedical model as a post-partum woman and mother, and (3) perceptions of media related to women's health and the health of children and families. This final chapter revisits themes of choice from chapter 1 as post-partum women make decisions about birth spacing and contraceptive methods.

Chapter 4 explores the intrinsic duality of the mother-child dyad to explicate how women make meaning of medicalization. These women resisted the biomedical paradigm in various ways, such as through trusting their bodies and valuing storytelling and personal narrative as a form of expertise.

The conclusion chapter summarizes the primary findings related to each body episode, including contraception, pregnancy, childbirth, and the postpartum period. This final chapter describes the importance of employing a "life course" perspective to address women's health and builds on a growing corpus of patient-centered public health literature by analyzing women's reproductive health across the lifespan.

## NOTES

1. Publisher's Note: The interviews used as supplemental research in this text were all conducted with the participants' knowledge and agreement that these interviews would be used in a later publication. Pseudonyms were used to protect the identities of participants.

## *Chapter One*

# Beyond "the Pill"

## *Integrating Body and Self*

In 2014, the term "birth control," coined by Planned Parenthood's® founder Margaret Sanger, turned 100 years old. Sanger (1919) argues:

> We maintain that a woman possessing an adequate knowledge of her reproductive functions is the best judge of the time and conditions under which her child should be brought into this world. We further maintain that it is her right, regardless of all other considerations, to determine whether she shall bear children or not, and how many children she shall bear if she chooses to become a mother. To this end we insist that information in regard to scientific contraceptives be made open to all. (11)

According to the Guttmacher Institute, more than 99% of reproductive-aged women who have ever had sexual intercourse have used at least one contraceptive method. The U.S. Centers for Disease Control and Prevention (CDC) recognize family planning as one of the ten great public health achievements of the twentieth century. The modern birth-control movement, founded by Sanger, offers women the opportunity to plan and space births (CDC 1999). Family planning improves maternal and infant health, enhances family and community well-being, and offers a host of societal benefits. Contraception empowers women and increases access to educational and professional opportunities.

College women, ages 18 to 24 years, have the highest rates of unintended pregnancies and induced abortions, which has largely been attributed to lack of contraceptive use. At least 80% of college females are sexually active and at risk of unintended pregnancy. This chapter provides a foundation for understanding female college students' knowledge, perceptions, and use of contraceptive methods. I present 18 in-depth interviews with young women ages 18 to 23 to explore their attitudes and perceptions of contraceptive options. Specifically, this chapter explores women's meaning making of contraception in three areas: (1) the physiological experience of contraception, (2) perceptions of medicine and the biomedical model surrounding contraception, and (3) perceptions of mediated messages about contraception.

## A BRIEF HISTORY OF CONTRACEPTION IN THE UNITED STATES

Since 1960, American women have been able to prevent pregnancy with the oral contraceptive pill. Despite widespread use of this highly effective form of birth control, approximately half of all pregnancies in the United States remain unintended. Almost 70% of pregnancies among young unmarried women ages 20 to 29 are unplanned. These unplanned pregnancies are associated with poor birth outcomes, decreased childhood health, maternal depression and other complications, as well as negative economic consequences. According to researchers and medical professionals, "societies in both the developing and developed world suffer from unacceptably high rates of unintended and unwanted pregnancies, despite the availability of safe and effective forms of contraception" (Sitruk-Ware, Nath, and Mishell 2013, 320).

The 2010 U.S. Patient Protection and Affordable Care Act (ACA) designated contraception as essential women's preventive health care and requires all new private health insurance plans to cover contraceptives approved by the Food and Drug Administration without cost sharing (Health Resources and Services Administration 2014). With the barrier of cost addressed, women may have greater access to contraception, including the most effective options (Eisenberg, McNicholas, and Peipert 2013; Rose et al. 2011). Despite this guarantee, recent research suggests that many insurers still fail to cover all FDA-approved contraceptive options without cost sharing, especially intrauterine devices (IUDs), hormonal patches, and vaginal rings (Sobel, Salganicoff, and Kurani 2015; Benyo et al. 2015). The history of contraceptive use offers insight into the struggle to reduce unintended pregnancy. See table 1.1 for a more detailed timeline of contraception in the United States.

In 1839, Charles Goodyear ushered in an era of modern contraception by vulcanizing rubber and manufacturing barrier contraceptive methods, such as condoms and diaphragms. Within thirty years, Americans had access to barrier methods, including condoms, sponges, diaphragms, and cervical caps. In 1873, the Comstock Act defined contraception as obscene and limited the dissemination of contraceptive devices (Tone 2002). Despite laws prohibiting the use of contraception, research continued and the first patent for an intrauterine device (IUD) emerged in 1895. In the June 1914 issue of *The Woman Rebel*, Margaret Sanger used the term "birth control" for the first time. In 1916, Sanger was arrested for opening the first birth control clinic in the United States. By the 1920s, women used grassroots tactics to promote contraception through seminars, home visits, fundraising, and policy reform (Foley 1999). According to Tone (1997), "women's demands for safe and legal birth control were part of their feminist critique of American society, a critique that tied maternal sexuality to continuing social, political, and economic subordination" (xix).

In 1921, Sanger founded the American Birth Control League, the precursor to the Planned Parenthood Federation of America. According to Gordon (1997),

> the struggle for birth control which emerged in the nineteenth century was not directed solely toward the legalization of certain information and technology. It was part of a feminist movement, challenging the subordination of women in sexuality particularly and in the family and society generally. From then on, the birth control movement, even when organizationally autonomous, has always reflected the historical strength and development of feminism. (147)

The Crane decision (1918) provided the foundation for Sanger to open the first legal clinic in 1923 to provide contraceptives for therapeutic purposes, including the prevention of life-threatening pregnancies.

The building blocks for hormonal contraception emerged in the 1940s when chemist Russell Marker discovered Mexican wild yams, *cabeza de negro,* could be used to develop synthetic progesterone. In the 1950s, Gregory Pincus and John Rock at the Worcester Foundation for Experimental Biology conducted a fertility study with 50 women to test hormonal contraception. In an effort to maintain a "natural" process, these researchers created the 21-day hormonal cycle, which caused withdrawal bleeding to mimic menstruation.

In 1957, the U.S. Food and Drug Administration (FDA) approved *Enovid* oral contraception to treat severe menstrual disorders, with the warning that it suppresses ovulation. Although laws in thirty states prohibited or restricted the counseling and sale of birth control, Planned Parenthood Federation of America operated 200 birth control clinics in the 1950s. As late as 1959, President Dwight Eisenhower refused to discuss contraception, arguing, "I cannot imagine anything more emphatically a subject that is not a proper political or governmental activity or function or responsibility" (Foley 1999, 99).

U.S. laws restricting access to contraception started to change in the 1960s. *Griswold v. Connecticut* (1965) established the use of contraception as intrinsic to a couple's right to privacy. The FDA approved the use of

Searle's *Enovid* as a "birth control pill" for the first time. Despite these advances, the United States made little progress in the research and development of new contraceptive methods (Jaffe 1973). Although a patent for the vaginal contraception ring was issued in 1970, the FDA approved the first vaginal ring over thirty years later, in 2001. The FDA rejected the medical committee's recommendation to approve the contraception shot in 1973. Despite safe use of the shot worldwide since 1969, this method was not available to women in the U.S. until 1992. According to the FDA, over 10 million U.S. women had used the oral contraceptive pill by the 1980s. Research and development produced low-dosage versions of "the pill," which varied levels of progesterone and estrogen during the 21-day regimen. Between 1990 and 2001, the FDA approved a range of contraceptive methods, such as the ring, the patch, the shot, and the implant.

Support for contraception is almost universal in the United States, including among women of all religious denominations. Among women who have ever had sexual intercourse, 99% of Catholics and Protestants have used a form of contraception (Jones and Dreweke 2011). Studies suggest a pattern of contraceptive use across the reproductive lifespan, beginning with the use of condoms at first sexual intercourse, the pill to prevent pregnancy, and sterilization after achieving a desired number of children (Mosher and Jones 2010). If a woman plans to have two children, she will need to use some form of contraception for up to thirty years (Guttmacher Institute 2014). Many women rely on condoms and the oral contraceptive pill as their main methods of birth control (Mosher and Jones 2010). In fact, four out of five women who have ever had sexual intercourse have taken "the pill" (Daniels, Mosher, and Jones 2013). Studies indicate that college-age women, in particular, associate contraception with "the pill" (Jones, Mosher, and Daniels 2012; Sundstrom 2012).

In April 2013, the FDA approved emergency contraception for over-the-counter (OTC), nonprescription use for women ages 15 and older. Emergency contraception or Plan B offers a concentrated dosage of one of the hormones found in the oral contraceptive pill (OCP) and provides protection from unintended pregnancy within 72 hours of sexual intercourse, with decreasing effectiveness up to five days (Trussell, Raymond, and Cleland 2013). Research indicates that women are familiar with a range of contraceptive methods; however, high rates of unintended pregnancy, method dissatisfaction, and discontinuation suggest that women's contraceptive needs continue to be unmet. Clinical trials are currently testing extended cycle vaginal birth control rings; transdermal contraception and antimicrobial sprays and gels; and male hormonal contraception.

## EVOLUTION OF BIRTH CONTROL

Discussions of contraception in recorded history emerge as early as the fourth century B.C. in Hippocrates' *Nature of Women*: "if a woman does not want to become pregnant, make as thick a mixture of beans and water as you

| | | |
|---|---|---|
| B.C. | | The father of modern medicine, Hippocrates and the ancient philosophers Aristotle and Plato played a distinctive role in current societal norms and values surrounding contraception and medicalized reproduction |
| 1800s | 1839 | Charles Goodyear invents the technology to vulcanize rubber and manufactures rubber condoms, intrauterine devices, and diaphragms |
| | 1870s | Barrier methods of contraception are available in America, including condoms, sponges, diaphragms and cervical caps |
| | 1873 | Congress passes the Comstock Act, which lists contraceptives as obscene and illict, making it a federal offense to disseminate them through the postal service or across state lines. |
| | 1895 | The first patent for an intra-uterine contraceptive device (IUD) is issued |
| 1900s | 1914 | Margaret Sanger coins the term "birth control" in the June 1914 issue of *The Woman Rebel*. |
| | 1916 | Margaret Sanger is arrested for opening the first U.S. birth control clinic in Brooklyn, New York |
| | 1918 | The Crane decision is the first legal ruling allowing birth control to be used for therapeutic purposes |
| 1920s | 1921 | Margaret Sanger establishes the American Birth Control League, the antecedent of the Planned Parent Federation of America |
| | 1923 | Following the Crane decision, Margaret Sanger opens the first legal birth control clinic in the U.S. to provide contraceptives for medical purposes, including the prevention of life-threatening pregnancies |
| 1930s | 1936 | In *U.S. vs. One Package*, the court rules that physicians can receive contraception via the mail unless prohibited by a specific local law. |
| 1940s | 1941 | Chemist Russell Marker uses Mexican wild yams known as *cabeza de negro* to make synthetic progesterone. Progesterone will become the basis for hormonal contraception. |
| | 1944 | Gregory Pincus founds a small, private laboratory in Shrewsbury, Massachusetts, the Worcester Foundation for Experimental Biology, to pursue research on hormonal contraception |
| 1950s | | The Planned Parenthood Federation of America runs 200 birth control clinics. Anti-birth control laws on the books in thirty states still prohibit or restrict counseling and sale of contraception. |
| | 1954 | Gregory Pincus and John Rock, M.D. begin the first human trials of hormonal contraception with 50 women, under the guise of a fertility study. The regimen still in use today is established where progesterone is administered for only 21 days, |

**Table 1.1**

| | | |
|---|---|---|
| | | followed by a 7-day break initiating withdrawal bleeding to mimic menstruation, which allows oral contraception to be seen as a "natural" process. |
| | 1956 | Rock and Pincus launch the first large-scale human clinical trials for oral contraception in San Juan, Puerto Rico |
| | 1957 | The FDA approves the use of Enovid for the treatment of severe menstrual disorders and requires the drug label to carry the warning that Enovid will suppress ovulation |
| | 1959 | President Dwight Eisenhower discussed contraception: "I cannot imagine anything more emphatically a subject that is not a proper political or governmental activity or function or responsibility" |
| 1960s | 1960 | FDA approves Searle's Enovid as a "birth control pill." |
| | 1965 | The U.S. Supreme Court in *Griswold v. Connecticut* strikes down the Connecticut law prohibiting the use of birth control as a violation of a couple's right to privacy |
| | 1969 | Women around the world begin using the contraception shot/injection |
| 1970s | | The first patent for the development of the vaginal contraception ring is issued |
| | 1972 | The U.S. Supreme Court in *Eisenstadt v. Baird* rules that a state cannot stand in the way of distribution of birth control to a single person and strikes down Massachusetts law prohibiting the sale of contraceptives to unmarried women |
| | 1973 | FDA rejects application for the contraception shot/injection, despite committee's recommendation for approval |
| 1980s | | FDA reports that 10.7 million American women use oral hormonal contraception. New versions of low-dosage oral contraceptives are introduced. These products vary the amount of progesterone and estrogen in the drug during the 21-day cycle. |
| 1990s | 1990 | FDA approves the first contraception implant/rod (the most recent version, Implanon® was approved in 2006) |
| | 1992 | FDA approves the contraception shot/injection (Depo-Provera®) |
| 2000s | 2001 | FDA approves the first vaginal contraception ring (NuvaRing®) and the first transdermal contraception patch (Ortho Evra®) for use by women in the United States |
| | 2015 | Current research focuses on extended cycle vaginal birth control rings; transdermal contraception and antimicrobial sprays and gels; and male hormonal contraception, among others |

This timeline was constructed through review of a variety of sources (Collins 2009; Foley 1999; Tone 2002; Upadhyay 2005).

**Table 1.1 (cont.)**

can, make her drink it, and she will not become pregnant for a year" (Lefkowitz and Fant 2005). Scholars suggest that these early accounts, which must have been ineffective, may point to a tradition of women's wisdom in preventing pregnancy. However, male writers, such as Hippocrates, may not have possessed first-hand knowledge of women's approaches to preventing pregnancy. According to Blundell (2001),

> the ideological view of the female as a child-bearing vessel may have been effective in suppressing the notion that motherhood was something that women might sometimes want to avoid, and it is possible that contraception was often practiced without men's knowledge. (108)

Although the first known use of the term birth emerged in the early thirteenth century, the term derived from Scandinavian origin encompassing such meanings as offspring, nature, and fate (The American Heritage Dictionary 2014). The verb *control* appeared in the early fourteenth century from the Latin root "contra," meaning against. The origin of these terms suggests that "birth control" implies "against nature" or "against fate." Understanding the history of this term may help to shed light on modern controversies.

Birth control was coined by Margaret Sanger in 1914 and is defined as "voluntary prevention of conception by a man or a woman through the use of contraceptive techniques" or simply "a contraceptive technique" (The American Heritage Dictionary 2014). Although family planning emerged as a euphemism for birth control, it is now commonly understood as a program designed to regulate the number and spacing of children in a family through the practice of contraception to improve quality of life and to curb population growth (The American Heritage Dictionary 2014). Initially, family planning programs met with strong opposition. According to Davis (1981),

> birth control—individual choice, safe contraceptive methods, as well as abortions when necessary—is a fundamental prerequisite for the emancipation of women. . . . The progressive potential of birth control remains indisputable. But in actuality, the historical record of this movement leaves much to be desired in the realm of challenges to racism and class exploitation. (202–203)

Current protests and political attacks on Planned Parenthood suggest that many still view birth control as "against fate."

The World Health Organization (WHO) and the World Bank led successful campaigns to promote family planning and reach the development goals of developing countries (Truss, Marshall, and Blair-Stevens 2010). The effective implementation of health communication campaigns employing diffusion of innovations theory led to the success of family planning programs in developing countries (Murphy 2004; Rogers et al. 1999; Vaughan and Rogers 2000). Murphy (2004) found that the diffusion of family planning has been successful in developing countries through mass media, community education programs, and health care provider training. Social marketing played an important role in this diffusion by promoting new family planning methods through the local and mass media, and working with pharmacies and vendors to distribute the products (Murphy 2004). Despite this success, the history of coerced contraception domestically and globally forces us to "acknowledge the justice of ensuring equal access to birth control for poor and minority women without denying the injustice of imposing birth control as a means of reducing their fertility" (Roberts 1997, 56–57).

In 1994, the International Conference on Population and Development "marked a great paradigm shift in the field of population and development, replacing a demographically driven approach to family planning with one that is based on human rights and the needs, aspirations, and circumstances of each woman" (Osotimehin 2012). In 2012, the United Nations described family planning as a universal human right (Greene, Joshi, and Robles 2012). The U.N. Population Fund's annual report indicated that contraception offers the opportunity to improve women's lives. According to the World Health Organization (2013), "promotion of family planning—and ensuring access to preferred contraceptive methods for women and couples—is essential to securing the well-being and autonomy of women, while supporting the health and development of communities."

## PREVENTING UNINTENDED PREGNANCY

*Healthy People 2020* provides evidence-based, national benchmarks to improve the health and well-being of women, infants, children, and families. The family planning objectives include increasing the proportion of pregnancies that are intended, improving access and use of highly effective contraception, and increasing birth spacing to 18 months. By 2020, the national objectives aim to increase intended pregnancies to 56%. Increasing the use of highly effective contraception offers an important opportunity to increase intended pregnancies. According to the Centers for Disease Control and Prevention (CDC), 85 out of 100 sexually active women who do not use a method of birth control will become pregnant over the course of one year. Long-acting reversible contraception (LARC) methods, including the intrauterine device (IUD) and the implant, are over 99% effective with typical and perfect use. With typical or everyday use, the oral contraceptive pill is 91% effective and the male condom is 82% effective in preventing pregnancy.

In 2012, the American College of Obstetricians and Gynecologists (ACOG) recommended long-acting reversible contraception (LARC), including the intrauterine device (IUD) and implant, as first-line pregnancy prevention for all reproductive-age women, including adolescents. In 2014, the American Academy of Pediatrics (AAP) recommended LARC as the best contraceptive choice for adolescents as well. Research shows that LARC options (i.e., the IUD and the implant) are safe, less costly over the long term, and more effective than oral contraception. Studies indicate that these methods are acceptable and satisfactory for most women, including college-age women. Despite a steady increase in use from 2.4% in 2002 to 8.5% in 2009, LARC methods have not yet fulfilled their promise to increase intended pregnancies (Finer, Jerman, and Kavanaugh 2012). Research indicates that female health care providers are significantly more likely to use long-acting reversible contraception (LARC) methods compared to the general population. A recent study found that approximately 42% of female family planning providers use LARC methods (Stern et al. 2015).

According to Takeshita (2012), there are 150 million IUD users worldwide and it is the fourth most used contraceptive method in the global north. In the United States, women born abroad are three times more likely to have used an IUD compared with women born in America (Daniels, Mosher, and Jones 2013). The history of the Dalkon Shield may contribute to Americans' reluctance to adopt LARC methods. The Dalkon Shield was an IUD distributed in the United States in the 1970s. By 1974, the manufacturer voluntarily discontinued sale of the product due to complications related to the design and manufacturing of the device. The Centers for Disease Control and Prevention (CDC) (1983) found that women using the Dalkon Shield had a 5-fold increased risk of pelvic inflammatory disease (PID) compared with women using other IUDs. Although the risk was clearly associated with one malfunctioning product, the damage to the reputation of the IUD persists today. According to Takeshita (2012), "feminist scholarship on the IUD has thus been limited to the critique of the device as a population control tool and analysis of the events around the Dalkon Shield" (8).

Between 2013 and 2015, the Food and Drug Administration (FDA) approved two new hormonal IUDs, Skyla and Liletta, which provide protection from unintended pregnancy for up to three years. Skyla was designed specifically for women who have not yet had children and Liletta is marketed as a more affordable contraceptive option. These IUDs are smaller than the Mirena and ParaGard IUDs, which have been marketed as "lifestyle drugs" toward women who already have children. According to Takeshita (2014),

> the representation of the lifestyle IUD, however, obscures the history of the device and the broad spectrum of bio-political interests that its development engaged along the way. . . . The historical trajectories . . . involved creating and reinforcing inequities among women of different races, classes, nationalities, ages, and levels of modernity. (243)

The recent increased availability of IUDs offers women new choices in contraceptive options. Yet, decades of reproductive coercion and perceptions of menstruation as "natural" continue to serve as barriers to uptake of IUDs.

The boom and bust phenomenon may help explain why LARC methods are not widely used in the United States. A new technology or drug may demonstrate an initial increase in uptake followed by a leveling off or fall in demand. Contraceptive scare, as a result of negative media publicity, may cause women to discontinue their contraceptive method (Boonstra et al. 2000). For example, a January 2014 Vanity Fair article titled "Danger in the Ring" asked, "is the contraceptive NuvaRing killing thousands?" Although the article by Marie Brenner provided only anecdotal evidence and misleading statistics from questionable sources, the magazine sensationalized the story as a "full investigation" leading critics to describe the article as fear mongering. The boom and bust phenomenon indicates that barriers to uptake of LARC methods include the news media, the desire for a perfect method of contraception, and other contributing factors.

Contraceptive scare has impacted how women perceive hormonal contraception and the risk of adverse health effects. In particular, narratives about the risk of contraception tend to disregard or downplay the risks of pregnancy and childbirth. Studies show that the use of any method of contraception "prevents more deaths from pregnancy and childbirth than are associated with method use" (Kost, Forrest, and Harlap 1991). In other words, any risks associated with contraceptive methods should be compared with the risks of pregnancy and childbirth. For young healthy nonsmokers using the OCP, the risk of death is 240 times lower than the risk of death related to pregnancy complications (Becker and Betstadt 2013). Despite the safety of OCPs, approximately half of women in a recent study incorrectly believed that hormonal contraception is more dangerous than pregnancy, specifically citing pulmonary embolism, cancer risk, and infertility (Becker and Betstadt 2013). Dr. Becker suggested that these results may be attributed to the media whereby "the risks of pregnancy, deemed such a natural and healthy process by society, get overshadowed by the highly publicized reports of contraceptive-related complications."

Recently, a number of large cohort studies revealed reduced rates of cancer among women who had ever used hormonal contraception (Hannaford et al. 2010) and lower overall risk of death among current and past users of hormonal contraception compared with nonusers (Vessey, Yeates, and Flynn 2010). In other words, hormonal contraception offers a net health benefit to users, in addition to pregnancy prevention. A recent study of LARC methods found that one-year pregnancy rates and outcomes (such as pregnancy complications) following discontinuation were comparable to women using no contraceptive method or barrier methods (Mansour et al. 2011). Another study found that long-term use of OCP lowered the risk of Down syndrome in children among women of advanced maternal age and may be protective against miscarriage by limiting ovulatory cycles (Nagy et al. 2013). These studies and many others indicate that hormonal contraception decreases the risk of certain cancers and improves fertility. Overall,

LARC offers the opportunity to improve women's health and decrease unintended pregnancy.

The trailblazing CHOICE project in St. Louis demonstrates that initiatives to increase uptake of highly effective, low maintenance contraception can dramatically decrease unplanned pregnancy (Peipert et al. 2011; Secura et al. 2014; Secura et al. 2011). In recent years, national and local health communication campaigns focus on increasing uptake of LARC methods to improve women's method satisfaction and reduce unplanned pregnancies. In 2011, the Ad Council, in partnership with the National Campaign to Prevent Teen and Unplanned Pregnancy, designed the first national multimedia public service campaign to help young women identify a method that best suits their life. Bedsider (bedsider.org) offers an interactive online and mobile Birth Control Support Network providing facts about all methods and recommending the IUD and implant. Local and regional campaigns, such as Choose Well: The South Carolina Contraceptive Access Campaign encourage women to "Keep Calm and LARC On" (Sundstrom et al. 2014).

## CONVERSATIONS WITH COLLEGE WOMEN ABOUT CONTRACEPTION

In-depth interviews were essential to gain a rich, detailed understanding of the role of contraception in the lives of young women. I developed a "conversational partnership" with participants, which provides freedom to explore new ideas and unexpected directions (Rubin and Rubin 2012). I met with women at on-campus locations convenient to the participants and interviews lasted approximately one hour. To develop rapport with participants, I first asked questions about their daily lives, personal health, and media use. Then, I guided participants to discuss contraceptive methods, including examples of when they discussed contraception with people in their lives, history and satisfaction with contraceptive options, and what is important to them when choosing a method of contraception. A semi-structured interview guide allowed participants to lead the discussion (Rubin and Rubin 2012). When questions were needed to guide the conversation, I asked:

- What comes to your mind when you hear the word "contraception"?
- How would you describe *(contraceptive method)* to a friend who didn't know much about it?
- Where do you hear about different methods of contraception?
- Who is your most trusted source of information about contraceptive use?
- Is there anything that would make contraception easier for you?

A total of 18 women between 18 and 23 years of age completed in-depth interviews. Initially, purposive sampling, or selecting individuals based on predetermined criteria, was used to recruit participants (Glaser and Strauss 1967). To maximize variation among participants, snowball or chain-referral sampling was used to recruit participants by asking each respondent to suggest other individuals who would be interested in talking with me. All participants were enrolled as students in a large, urban, public university located in the Mid-Atlantic region of the United States. Participants included first year, sophomore, junior, and senior status. Student majors included Communication, Journalism, Economics, Psychology, Public Health, and English. Of the participants, 7 lived on campus, 3 lived in sorority houses, and 8 lived off campus. Women of all races, ethnicities, sexual orientations, religions, and abilities were eligible to participate. Participants were mostly white/Caucasian (14); however, some individuals self-identified as Asian–American (1), Black (1), Hispanic/Latina (1), and Asian (1).

Participants permitted their interview to be recorded and transcribed for detailed analysis. Participants also completed a brief, anonymous demographic survey. Participants were recruited throughout data collection until a point of theoretical saturation emerged in which no new concepts emerged from the interviews (Glaser and Strauss 1967). Analytical techniques from grounded theory methodology, including a constant-comparative method, provided an inductive approach to data collection and analysis to identify emerging concepts (Corbin and Strauss 2008). Memos and observer comments revealed and addressed my assumptions and biases as the researcher and helped me to maintain reflexivity (Rubin and Rubin 2012). Open and axial coding were used during data analysis to identify and relate concepts and themes across the data (Berg 2009).

## EXPERIENCING CONTRACEPTION: "THE PILL" AS THE NORM

Despite the ubiquity of "the pill," 73% of pregnancies among unmarried women aged 20 to 24 are unintended (Zolna and Lindberg 2012). Although the American College of Obstetricians and Gynecologists and the American Academy of Pediatrics recommend long-acting reversible contraceptive options, including the IUD and the implant, as safe and effective for young women and adolescents, these methods have not been widely adopted. In a recent article, I described how young women define birth control as "the pill," and social norms, health uncertainty, and limited knowledge emerged as barriers to use of nondaily contraceptive options (Sundstrom 2012). In this section, I expand on these findings to describe how and why young women rely on the OCP and resist LARC options.

### *The Importance of "Pill" Pressure*

Participants described the OCP as "the cultural norm" and "more common" among friends and family. One young woman said, "I know more people taking the pill. I've heard more firsthand stories." In other words, these young women valued personal experience and the social norm in their social network. Many participants also cited the noncontraceptive benefits of hormonal contraception and incorrectly believed that these positive side effects were limited to the OCP. According to one participant, "[the pill] is widely used because it is effective with regulating the menstrual cycle, helps with cramps, and clears up your skin." Nationally, 58% of pill users cite noncontraceptive health benefits, including treatment for excessive menstrual bleeding, menstrual pain, and acne as reasons for using the method (Jones 2011). Scholars suggest that "the pill" has been marketed as a lifestyle drug for these secondary effects since the 1990s (Jones 2011).

Beliefs about the effectiveness of the OCP revealed underlying social norms. One participant said, "my friends love the pill. It is a free pass to not get pregnant." Participants incorrectly believed that the pill was the most effective contraceptive method citing statistics of 99%, 99.9%, or 100% effective at preventing pregnancy. According to the Centers for Disease Control and Prevention (CDC), the OCP is only 91% effective with typical use. To these young women, the ubiquity of the OCP meant that it must be the most effective. One participant said "most people take the pill. I would think it's the most effective." Another young woman agreed, "[LARC methods] must be less effective because they are not as popular [as the pill]." These young women emphasized the importance of responsibility and believed they could control the effectiveness of the OCP. Participants said, "all the methods are the same effectiveness—if you do them right," "when used properly, they are all equally effective," and "the effectiveness is all the same if they are maintained correctly." Despite this confidence in the OCP, most young women could identify an example of a woman becoming pregnant while on the pill. According to one participant, "I know plenty of people who got pregnant while on the pill." Another young woman said, "they've come a long way in preventing STDs and pregnancies, but nothing is fool proof."

Participants negotiated perceptions of responsibility and control with stories of unintended pregnancy while on the OCP. According to one young woman, "my mom got pregnant with me on birth control. She took it every day and was not on antibiotics." Another participant said, "I've heard of the pill not working. But I have always taken it well. I had a friend who got pregnant and had twins while taking the pill. She had taken it every day and it still happened." Although stories about the failure of the OCP, despite perfect adherence, were common among participants, these young women believed that they could control the effectiveness of "the pill." One participant summarized this perspective: "the pill is something that I can be in control of, which is important to me. I am diligent and I remember to take it every day."

At the same time, many participants described forgetting to take the OCP everyday. One participant said:

> My only complaint about the pill is that it's a little annoying to take it every day. I set an alarm on my phone to remind me. Some of my friends take it in the morning or at night. I don't think other people are as serious as I am about taking it at the same time every day. I have gotten so used to it, I always take it around the same time every day. It makes me more comfortable because I am in control and I know it is working because I am taking it the same every day.
>
> [Have you ever forgotten to take the pill?]
>
> It's happened before—I've forgotten a few days. But, I still take it seriously. And my phone alarm is a good reminder.

Participants described the risks of missing a pill: "taking the pill is uncomfortable because you have to stay to a schedule. If you forget, people freak out because it doesn't work the same." Another participant said, "a lot of people forget [to take their pill]. Especially in college, your lifestyle doesn't make it easy to take at same time every day. I set an alarm on my phone." Despite understanding the risk of unintended pregnancy participants were more likely to perceive the OCP as risky for others, who were described as forgetful or less serious. A participant said:

> My roommate always forgets to take her pill. She doesn't set a phone alarm. We always talk about how we're bad about taking it. I set an alarm on my phone but if I ever leave my purse at home, that's really bad. But, usually I'm not worried about it. Only if I miss like a Thursday and then go on a weekend trip without it, that's not great.

Another young woman said, "I've forgotten to take the pill before. I won't remember until the next day. So, I take that pill and the next day's pill. And I know there's no chance I could get pregnant."

The marketing of the OCP may influence young women's perceptions of safety. Most participants agreed, "the pill seems the most safe because it doesn't go in you. You just swallow it and you're done." Many of these young women shared the perception that "the pill is natural. It is an every day thing." However, some participants disagreed. According to one young woman, "the pill is not natural regulation. I don't like it. It may cause problems once you stop taking it. You could have problems, like with your period being irregular." Another participant agreed, "pills can cause a long-term effect and people don't realize the negative aspects of it." Some participants believed that contraception could increase risk of cancer or infertility, especially if you used it for a "long period." According to one young woman,

"I've been told you should avoid being on birth control for more than five years."

These fears were magnified in relation to Plan B and long-acting reversible contraceptive (LARC) methods. According to one participant, "Plan B doesn't seem like the best thing for you." Participants believed that emergency contraception or Plan B was "only for an emergency" and "should not be relied on as a contraceptive method." According to one participant, "I don't consider Plan B a contraceptive. It is an alternative. You're not supposed to take it all the time. It will stop working the more you take it." These young women indicated that emergency contraception was not as effective as the OCP and many participants suggested that they didn't think of it as contraception. In summary, these young women believed that "Plan B is a more serious measure, it is a higher dose of hormones."

In a similar way, participants described LARC methods as "aggressive," "intense," and "a little scary." One young woman said, "the IUD hurts to get it. It is scary. I would not do that." Another participant said, "sometimes the IUD grows into the body and people forget to check it." In addition to physical concerns, participants expressed social concerns about the implications of using LARC methods. According to one young woman, "if a girl uses the IUD she might be promiscuous. People feel that the IUD is a radical method, so, you wouldn't need it unless you were having a lot of sex." Other participants couldn't identify exactly why they were averse to these methods, "there is something I don't like about [LARC]."

A lack of awareness of the IUD influenced perceptions of safety among these young women. According to one participant, "I don't know about the IUD. There is not enough out there. I'm assuming because it's new. If it's new there are not enough studies, what the implications might be." According to another young woman,

> I know that there are other options, like the IUD. Americans tend to avoid it, but it's popular with Europeans. I'm still skeptical. Even though I understand it. It just feels riskier. It seems very new. It is invasive and requires going to a doctor. Somehow, the risks are terrifying. That's my gut reaction.

Many participants described LARC methods as an option after having children. According to one participant, "I might consider the IUD after I had kids. If I wanted a break between kids, I would possibly consider it." Another young woman concurred, "I would possibly use the implant later on, if I don't know if I want to have more kids, it would be a viable method."

Participants wanted to know, "is it easy?" "is it going to hurt?" "if there is a complication, do I have to go to the doctor?" One participant said, "I would consider the IUD because once you have it, it is convenient, you don't need to worry about it. But it's not 100% safe, you can still lose it inside and you can have problems with it." Control over their contraceptive method, including discontinuation, was important to these young women. A recent study found that the majority of women were interested in IUD self-removal and were more likely to recommend this method when they learned about the option of self-removal (Foster et al. 2014). Some participants were interested in pursuing a LARC method. According to one young woman, "the IUD, the implant—you can't really screw them up." Another participant agreed, "I am seriously considering the IUD because it is the most effective and I am not willing to settle. It is also easy to use and requires less maintenance."

### *The Meaning of Menstruation*

Participants' understanding of menstruation and withdrawal bleeding influenced their perceptions of LARC methods. Most participants desired a "natural" cycle with moderation (Sundstrom 2012). Many participants were comfortable "planning out when I get my period" by skipping pill-free intervals. This is consistent with extant research, in which 73% of women in a recent study had ever skipped pill-free intervals and 38% regularly altered their cycle (Picavet 2014). Another recent study among university college-aged women found increasing numbers of young women who alter withdrawal bleeding in favor of less frequent cycles (Lakehomer et al. 2013).

Research shows that there is no medical reason for women to have a monthly pill-free interval, which causes withdrawal bleeding (Hillard 2014; Picavet 2014). A Cochrane Database Systematic Review supports the safety of continuous use of hormonal contraception, which may offer improved compliance, increased satisfaction, fewer menstrual symptoms, and less menstruation-related absences (Edelman et al. 2014). Furthermore, "although pharmaceutical companies, instead of women, led the way with their new products, the idea that a woman could suppress her menstruation to free herself from an unnecessary burden has taken hold among consumers" (Takeshita 2014, 253).

Despite the advantages to avoiding the pill-free interval, some participants in this study resisted menstrual suppression. This may have been related to the belief that withdrawal bleeding was the same as menstruation. One participant said:

> Different forms of the pill, such as Seasonale, where you only get your period every 3 or 4 months, are not as popular. People who are sexually active want to get their period. They want a monthly, regular cycle, every time. They are reassured every month that the pill is fully effective.

Participants found a "regular cycle" reassuring, even though withdrawal bleeding is unrelated to pregnancy. While some participants simply "don't have a problem with having a period," others displayed suspicion of contraceptive methods. One young woman said, "Seasonale® is insane. The body is made up a certain way, works a certain way. Birth control says it doesn't affect children, but Seasonale® decreases your chances of having children."

The meaning of menstruation continues to be debated by women, feminists, and scholars. According to Aengst and Layne (2014), "from a liberal feminist perspective, eliminating menstruation would be beneficial" in order to increase women's individual choice (181). In 2007, the Society for Menstrual Cycle Research stated, "it is the position of the Society that menstruation is not a disease, and that further research on the potential health risks and long-term safety of cycle-stopping contraception is still needed" (Hitchcock and Johnston-Robledo 2007). In an effort to facilitate this research, in 2014, the Society for Menstrual Cycle Research launched a new journal in partnership with Taylor & Francis/Routledge titled *Women's Reproductive Health*.

Rock and Pincus, the creators of the oral contraceptive pill, developed the 21-day hormonal cycle to mirror the "natural" process of menstruation. Coutinho and Segal (1999) describe the cultural significance of menstruation, arguing that dosage regimens mimic natural cycles because women may relate menstruation with femininity and monthly bleeding assuages fears of pregnancy. From an evolutionary perspective, up until the demographic transition from high birth and death rates to low birth and death rates, most women experienced many pregnancies and lactational amenorrhea due to long stretches of breastfeeding. According to Strassmann (1999), most women in a pre-industrial society menstruated about one hundred times in their life compared to an average of three hundred and fifty to four hundred times for the average American woman today.

Modern diseases, such as ovarian and endometrial cancer, may be the consequence of women menstruating up to four hundred times (Gladwell 2000). Coutinho and Segal (1999) argue that we live in an age of incessant menstruation that is not "natural" and may increase clinical disorders such as anemia, endometriosis, and pre-menstrual syndrome (PMS). According to Gladwell (2000),

> the Pill is really only natural in so far as it's *radical*–rescuing the ovaries and endometrium from modernity. That Rock insisted on a twenty-eight-day cycle for his pill is evidence of just how deep his misunderstanding was: the real promise of the Pill was not that it could preserve the menstrual rhythms of the twentieth century but that it could disrupt them.

## *Messages about Contraception*

The media impacted young women's perceptions of contraception directly and indirectly. In particular, participants perceived commercials about the IUD to cater to an "older generation" and women who already had children. This perception may have impacted understandings of effectiveness. According to one participant, "I think all birth control is supposed to work the same. They don't advertise what works better than another method." This is an important opportunity for health communicators and health care providers to address young women's misconceptions about the OCP and LARC methods.

Participants relied on personal experience and the stories of women in their social network. According to one young woman "I ask around to find out about people's experiences. I think that is just as helpful as the facts." Another participant said, "I want to hear from someone I trust and personally know, who has used the method." These young women primarily discussed contraception with friends and family members. According to one participant, "I take suggestions from my friends, then I look it up on the Internet. I Google it." Another young woman said, "I would Google in the first place." Many young women described talking with their mothers about the IUD, many of which believed that the IUD was unsafe. According to one participant, "I talked to my mom, I definitely had a conversation with her, and she said the IUD was terrifying and unnecessary."

Many participants did not know anyone who had used an IUD. Without personal stories from individuals in their social network, young women were unlikely to choose a LARC method. According to one participant, "even if the doctor told me about [a LARC method], I would still want to be on something that we know enough about, in terms of side effects and safety." Many participants described a similar approach by health care providers, who did not discuss LARC options, instead saying, "I'm going to go ahead and write a prescription for the pill." Most participants believed that "my doctor didn't sit me down and discuss my options." Participants trusted Planned Parenthood and visited these health centers to access birth control with friends, and during the high school years. One young woman said, "Planned Parenthood has always been there for me."

## CONCLUSION

More than 99% of reproductive-aged women who have ever had sexual intercourse have used at least one contraceptive method. Title X and Medicaid provide family planning services to women and men of reproductive age. These publicly supported family planning services averted 2.2 million unintended pregnancies and resulted in net government savings of $13.6 billion in 2010, or $7.09 for every public dollar spent (Frost et al. 2014). In 2014, the U.S. federal government provided quality family planning recommendations for the first time. The report was developed by the CDC and the Office of Population Affairs (OPA) of the U.S. Department of Health and Human Services (HHS). The recommendations outline quality family planning services, including contraception (Gavin, Moskosky, and Carter 2014).

In order to achieve the 2020 national objective to increase intended pregnancies to 56%, researchers and practitioners need to address method dissatisfaction and discontinuation in order to meet women's contraceptive needs. Increasing the use of highly effective contraception offers an important opportunity to increase intended pregnancies. A number of misconceptions must be addressed before more women will choose a long-acting reversible method of contraception. Messages about LARC should emphasize the safety of continuous use of hormonal contraception including decreasing the risk of certain cancers and improving fertility. The noncontraceptive benefits of these options should also be addressed. In other words, risks must be reconceptualized outside of the normative "natural" processes of menstruation, pregnancy, and childbirth. According to Haraway (2004), "'nature' and 'realism' are precisely the consequences of representational practices. Where we need to move is not 'back' to nature, but elsewhere, through and within an artifactual social nature" (90).

The persistence of duality in Western culture, such as mind/body and male/female, perpetuate the oppression of women and people of color, while technology offers an opportunity to problematize these dualisms (Haraway 2004). It is within this tension that women come to understand and interpret their bodies. In society, how does the focus on prevention contribute to the medicalization of pregnancy? When we study "preventing unintended pregnancy," are we implicitly suggesting that we need to prevent pregnancy like we prevent disease? Do prevention messages distort the reality of reproduction? In what ways do these mediated messages of contraception construct knowledge about reproduction? In order to understand these questions, we must explore the meanings of reproduction, pregnancy, and the body further.

# *Chapter Two*

# (Re)writing the Body

## *(Re)producing Pregnancy*

Divergent views of pregnancy as a normal part of women's reproductive life cycle compared to pregnancy as pathology in need of medical intervention developed in the ancient era and continue today (Rooks 1999). The midwifery model of care understands pregnancy as a significant social and physiological process imbued with meaning. According to Rooks (1999),

> a large part of the midwife's attention and concern focus on the woman as a person, a unique individual, in the context of her family and her life. The midwife is interested in the woman's expectations and experience of her pregnancy—her perceptions and beliefs; her knowledge, opinions, questions, and worries; her feelings, satisfactions and dissatisfactions, comforts and discomforts; her desires, decisions and actions, and the effect of all of these on her pregnancy; the development of her fetus; her labor, delivery, breastfeeding, and postpartum recovery; and how she mothers her infant. In these realms, as well as in understanding the process of normal birth, midwives have made unique contributions to the body of knowledge about human reproduction. (126–127)

Historically, the profound role of midwives in the lives of women and families led to suspicion.

Midwives became a target of the Inquisition in Europe during the fifteenth and sixteenth centuries. Scholars estimate that 80% of the 60,000 individuals executed as witches were women and more than half of those were midwives (Rooks 1999; Siegemund 2005; Ehrenreich and English 2010).

During the colonial period in the United States, midwives were responsible for the care of pregnant women. Since pregnancy and childbirth were not understood as diseases, these topics were omitted from early medical education until doctors realized the potential for obstetrics as a highly profitable specialty. According to Rooks (1999), "many doctors wanted to develop a larger role in childbirth. By the end of the 1700s, obstetrics had developed into a medical specialty and was taught in medical schools" (15). Although physicians attended nearly half of all births in the United States by 1900, midwives continued to play an important role in rural communities. According to Smith (1995), "although black midwives were part of the rural poor, they were highly prestigious members of the communities they served. They were respected health care experts and played an important role in cultural transmission and community leadership" (119).

The history of midwifery compared to the biomedical paradigm offers historical context to understand how pregnant women make meaning of their body. In a postmodern context, the body is not an object but rather the medium through which human beings experience the world. The unwarranted distinction or separation of the body as something owned, operated, or in any way outside of the self infringes on understandings of the self. According to Sartre, "I *am* my body, not that I *have* a body" (Moran 2000). This distinction is significant for research into current perceptions of the body and the self. The personal distinction between self and body allows societal norms around the female body to prevail. According to Moran (2000), "Sartre's account of the non-presence of self to self is an important forerunner of Derrida's conception of différance" (390). Derrida's concept of différance reflects the French verb différer, which means both "to differ" and "to defer." That concept permeates the notion of self and the "other" with meanings of difference and deference, particularly in the case of subgroups to the dominant cultural group, which exercises hegemony. Within this power dynamic, women might reclaim their bodies and empower themselves culturally through the singular action of personifying themselves and their bodies as one.

Merleau-Ponty describes the dialectic of the body, sexuality, and otherness as a philosophy of embodiment (Moran 2000). Women's reproductive health focuses on this triad of gendered identity: body, sexuality, and otherness. In particular, the discussion of the body as more than the sum of its parts can be applied to the medicalization and pathologizing of women's bodies. William Hunter (1774) illustrated the *Anatomy of the Human Gravid Uterus,* which featured a pregnant woman's open, dismembered torso showing the fetus (complete with a head of hair). This graphic depiction of the pregnant woman and fetus provides a picture of the medicalization of pregnancy. By displaying the pregnant woman as simply a uterus, the illustration suggests that the woman is not more than the sum of her parts. Merleau Ponty describes this as "partes extra partes" or parts outside parts and indicates that when an organism is viewed outside the context of its environment, it is essentialized and broken down to its component parts (Moran 2000). This lack of an embodied dialectic is the cornerstone of the medicalizing and pathologizing of women's bodies.

The current research and analysis of gender, fertility, and the body substantiates the need for further inquiry into the social constructs that contribute to the understanding of the female body before, during, and after pregnancy. The study of the unique phenomenon of pregnancy has significance for the overall study of gender and the body as well as the specific inquiry into gender, pregnancy, and the body. Is it possible for women to (re)produce what they have learned about preventing pregnancy in order to (re)write their experiences of living in the body? What is the lived experience of medicalized reproduction? In other words, what is the lived experience of pregnancy in a culture of prevention? In what ways do women negotiate cultural and social meanings of reproduction in order to "live in the body?" In this chapter, I present the results of in-depth interviews with 19 pregnant women ages 24 to 38 to understand their perceptions of pregnancy. This chapter uncovers pregnant women's body identity, perceptions, and opportunities for empowerment and agency.

## RE(WRITING) THE BODY

The discourse surrounding fertility, gender, and the body emphasizes the significance of social and cultural norms, as well as learned behaviors and meanings on the decision(s) to become pregnant, the experience(s) of being pregnant, and the discussions of the body and female embodiment. The first known use of the term *pregnant* emerged in the fourteenth century, derived from Middle English and originally from the Latin *praegnant*-and *praegnans*, meaning to carry a fetus, which is an alteration of *praegnas,* from *prae*- pre- and *-gnas* (akin to *gignere* to give birth to) (Merriam-Webster 2004, 979). In other words, pregnancy means "before giving birth to." It is a temporary state, which exists for the sole purpose of "giving birth to." This understanding of pregnancy leaves a fundamental question unanswered: "giving birth to" whom? The subject of this sentence is notably absent, reinforcing the fundamental tension between self and identity in pregnancy.

Sevón (2005) illustrates that the timing of motherhood represents social and cultural narratives around "good" mothering and a "reasonable" female life course. Female gender roles and identity, particularly for heterosexual females that are married, are bound by the social norms that dictate when and how "good" pregnancies occur. The decision to become pregnant, then, becomes a reflection of the female's heterosexual relationship and her "duties" therein (Sevón 2005). Bailey's (1999) research furthers the discussion of norms and the pregnant female body and concludes that while women may be somewhat excused from aspects of their identity in the process of pregnancy, they continue to be subjectified. This analysis confirms the notion that pregnancy may be studied as a unique phenomenon but may not be separated from the gender constructs of the prevailing social norms.

Warren and Brewis (2004) concur with the socially constructed phenomenon, arguing that pregnancy represents a body episode that reveals the Western idea of control over the body. The uniqueness of the female experience in pregnancy breaks with the pervasive perception that women have control over their body and should conform to the cultural stereotypes of womanhood and beauty. This "body episode" presents frustration for women who are unable to relinquish that perception of control while emancipating other women, for the brief period of pregnancy, to live outside of the cultural expectations for the female body. According to Butler (2010),

> the female body that is freed from the shackles of the paternal law may well prove to be yet another incarnation of that law, posing as subversive but operating in the service of that law's self-amplification and proliferation. . . . The culturally constructed body will then be liberated, neither to its "natural" past, nor to its original pleasures, but to an open future of cultural possibilities. (126–127)

Through language, sex education, and cultural norms, women's identity is challenged throughout the life course. Throughout their lives, women experience a fragmented self in their responsibility to prevent pregnancy, and perhaps later, through their desire for a pregnancy. The transition from preventing pregnancy to creating pregnancy is often wrought with anxiety and uneasiness because this change requires a fundamental challenge to self-identity. In this way, women experience a fragmented identity: who they were when they successfully prevented pregnancy, and a new self that is in some ways defined by a biological, reproductive role. In these terms, in the structure we have created for women, the act of pregnancy, by definition, requires the relinquishing of control. Haraway (2004) offers hope that women may reappropriate modern technology to address these dichotomies, "a cyborg world might be about lived social and bodily realities in which people are not afraid of their joint kinship with animals and machines, not afraid of permanently partial identities and contradictory standpoints" (13).

Pregnant women literally experience "the existence of an inner life," which in many ways denies the validity of a personal self-identity. Social norms dictate that pregnant women change their behavior: no drinking, no smoking, and no caffeine. At the end of the journey of a planned pregnancy, women's identity is split yet again, as she becomes a "mother." Modern euphemisms for "pregnant" include expecting, in a family way, and in a delicate condition. Although the word "pregnant" meaning "with child" emerged in the 1540s, it was likely used about one hundred years earlier in figurative senses. This gap reflects its status as a taboo word, which persisted until the twentieth century. Around the 1800s, slang terms for "pregnant" included "poisoned," in reference to the swelling (Merriam-Webster 2004, 979).

Today, the word "pregnant" can be defined in a number of ways, including the normative definition, "containing a developing embryo, fetus, or unborn offspring within the body," but also "having possibilities of development or consequence," "involving important issues," "rich in significance or implication," and even "abounding in fancy, wit, or resourcefulness" (Merriam-Webster 2004, 979). These definitions imply that through pregnancy and the bearing of heirs, women achieve richness of significance. Furthermore, the feminine qualities of fancy, wit, and resourcefulness are associated with pregnancy. In this way, women achieve their full societal possibility and cultural importance through reproducing.

According to Friedan (2001),

> it is historical, political reality that when motherhood was women's only function, status and identity, as well as her biological necessity, it kept her, or was used as an excuse to keep her, from education or opportunity to use her abilities in the mainstream of our evolving society. The inequality of woman, her second-class status in society, was in historical reality linked to that biological state of motherhood. (90)

This philosophy provides a lens to critique essentialism of women's bodies. This lens is supplemented by Merleau-Ponty's phenomenological account of "being-in-the-world." Merleau-Ponty offers a "very challenging and complex account of what he sees as the 'mysterious,' 'paradoxical,' 'ambiguous' nature of our embodiment in a world which seems pre-ordained to meet and fulfill our meaning-intending acts" (Moran 2000, 391). Merleau-Ponty sought to move beyond duality, to evolve past subject-object and soul-body dialectics. In this way, he urged scholars to abandon traditional philosophical dualisms and deal directly with the problem of intersubjectivity (Moran 2000, 401).

Through this lens, the medicalization and pathologizing of women's bodies begins before we are able to recognize it. It is a common refrain: "women spend half of their lives preventing pregnancy." With the help of comprehensive sex education and Title X, young women learn that the "responsible" way to "control" their bodies is through contraception. Ideally, girls are educated, empowered, and guided toward safe sex, in order to prevent sexually transmitted infections and pregnancy. This dual responsibility gives young women the impression that they can control their bodies by avoiding pregnancy.

Although concealed in empowering language, "safe sex" reduces women to their component parts. According to van Manen (2007), "in my native Dutch language the word for womb is baarmoeder, literally 'mother who bears,' mother who holds, carries the child. So both childbearing and giving birth are aspects of the same verb 'to bear'" (60). Women's reproductive organs are thereby linked to the role of "mother." This is problematic for women's identities for two reasons. First, the ability to reproduce does not determine the desire or ability to be a "mother." Second, the inability to reproduce does not limit the desire or ability to be a "mother," or one who "holds the child." Ultimately, the focus on preventing pregnancy obscures and limits women's understanding of what it really means to live in the body.

## (RE)PRODUCING PREGNANCY

A feminist, qualitative approach was essential to gain a rich and nuanced understanding of pregnancy in the lives of women. I conducted in-depth interviews with women in locations where they felt most comfortable talking with me, such as coffee shops, office locations, or the participants' homes. Interviews lasted between one hour to over one and a half hours. To develop rapport with participants, I first asked questions about their daily routines and what they like to do. Then, an open-ended discussion guide facilitated conversation during the interviews. The questions uncovered perceptions of pregnancy, including becoming pregnant, feelings about the body during pregnancy, expectations and decision making about pregnancy, and work-life changes during pregnancy. When questions were needed to guide the conversation, I asked:

- What is it like to be pregnant?
- What medical prenatal care, if any, have you had?
- Where do you seek information or advice regarding pregnancy?
- Do you remember seeing anything in the media telling you what to do as a pregnant woman?

I conducted 19 in-depth interviews with pregnant women between the ages of 24 and 38. These women were between 15 and 37 weeks pregnant at the time of the interview. Of the participants, 14 were experiencing their first pregnancy, while 5 already had one child. Most participants self-identified as white (89%), and 2 participants self-identified as African American/biracial. All participants reported an undergraduate degree, and 9 participants earned a graduate degree. I used purposive and theoretical sampling to recruit participants through informal contacts and acquaintances (Corbin and Strauss 2008). Theoretical sampling based on concepts aims to improve maximum variation, which facilitates identification of outliers and deviant cases in order to contextualize patterns (Miles and Huberman 1994). To increase transferability of conclusions, a purposive sampling strategy included women of different ages, different stages of pregnancy and parity, as well as women experiencing different contextual factors, such as fertility treatments. A point of theoretical saturation in the data was reached after 19 interviews, when no new concepts emerged (Glaser and Strauss 1967).

Participants permitted their interview to be recorded and transcribed for detailed analysis. Participants also completed a brief, anonymous demographic survey. Analytical techniques from grounded theory methodology, including a constant-comparative method, provided an inductive approach to data collection and analysis to identify emerging concepts (Corbin and Strauss 2008). Memos and observer comments revealed and addressed my assumptions and biases as the researcher and helped me to maintain reflexivity (Rubin and Rubin 2012). Open and axial coding were used during data analysis to identify and relate concepts and themes across the data (Berg 2009).

### *Pregnancy as a Surprise*

In 2003, actress Brooke Shields announced that she was pregnant with her second child. She said that the pregnancy was a "huge surprise" for her and husband Chris Henchy. They conceived their first child, daughter Rowan, through *in vitro* fertilization (IVF) and were preparing to "start" on fertility treatment when she learned she was pregnant. The "surprise" pregnancy has become a common trope among celebrities and in pop culture. In the popular HBO drama *Sex and the City*, character Charlotte tries acupuncture and fertility treatment before adopting a daughter. In the *Sex and the City Movie*, Charlotte finds herself unexpectedly pregnant, having conceived naturally despite an infertility diagnosis.

Women experience pregnancy as a surprise (Sundstrom 2013). In this section, I expand on this finding to illustrate cultural narratives of appropriate reproduction. With each of the women that I talked to about pregnancy, an element of "surprise" emerged. One participant described pregnancy as "new life and kind of a surprise. It's like getting a package and not knowing what is inside." In literature, anagnorisis, or discovery, is the protagonist's sudden recognition of her own or another character's true identity or nature. Through this technique, previously unforeseen character information is revealed. Anagnorsis originated in Ancient Greek theater as a moment in a play or other work when a character makes a critical discovery. Anagnorisis originally meant recognition in its Greek context, not only of a person but also of what that person stood for. It was the hero's sudden awareness of a situation, the realization of things as they stood, and finally, the hero's insight into a relationship. In this way, the lived experience of pregnancy as a surprise may be viewed as a modern awakening to the understanding and implications of the biological, reproductive role.

Participants understood intended pregnancy as a spectrum. Some participants employed technologies, including *in vitro* fertilization (IVF), ovulation predictor kits, or pharmaceutical drugs to induce ovulation, such as Clomid. Other participants described "leaving themselves open to" pregnancy by using less effective birth control options, such as the fertility awareness method, while others simply "stopped preventing" pregnancy by discontinuing hormonal contraception. Still other participants described "trying" to become pregnant by tracking their most fertile periods, often aided by a mobile phone application. According to one participant, "I really did adhere to the schedule on my app. So it was a really detailed schedule and it had the best days."

According to another participant, her pregnancy "was a surprise and not necessarily a pleasant one. . . . We had been wanting to not have kids for awhile but still kind of left ourselves open to it because we were using natural family planning or fertility awareness." Another participant described the uncertainty surrounding conception:

> There was a lot of uncertainty, a lot of you know, "are we doing the right thing?" "Are we doing it correctly?" "Are we gonna get pregnant?" and "*How can we get pregnant*?" A lot of just this worry, "is our timing right?" And you worry, "if I don't get pregnant this month, how long is it going to take?" In between trying and finding out you're pregnant, there's a lot of uncertainty too. Like one of the things I did is I bought a box of pregnancy tests and I took one maybe a couple of weeks after I thought I might be able to find out and it was negative and so it was like, "oh no, we have to start this all over again." But like a week or two later, I just felt kind of off, I can't even explain it, and so I took another test and I was pregnant. So yeah a lot of just uncertainty, "am I pregnant, am I not?"

Another participant described the surprise of pregnancy as a turnaround because she had convinced herself that she was not pregnant:

> We chose to just sort of stop preventing, so we didn't start taking my temperature or doing any ovulation kits or anything. When we were ready, we said okay, if it happens it happens. . . . Part of the reason is because I think my mom, when I was growing up, always told me be careful in having sex, make sure that you don't think that you can have sex, even once, without protection and not get pregnant. So, knowing this ahead of time, plus being impatient made me think that okay I'm going to get pregnant right away. Luckily, I did, but I didn't think I was, which is funny, because after the first month I thought it hadn't worked. . . . I didn't think I was, I'm not sure, I hadn't gotten my period, but I think I was assuming I would.

Surprise is commonly understood as a sudden, unexpected event. This definition is at odds with the experience of planned pregnancy. However, a secondary definition of surprise is the astonishment you feel when something totally unexpected happens to you. It is a type of modification, alteration, or change. While pregnancy is not unexpected, it is certainly a modification, alteration, or change. Further, a surprise can be defined as an event that occurs when something passes from one state or phase to another. For some women, pregnancy may be defined as the temporary state or transition from "woman" to "mother."

### *Pregnancy as a Secret*

Georgina Chapman, founder and designer of the successful fashion label Marchesa discussed her recent pregnancy with Derek Blasberg (2011):

> Initially, she worried how pregnancy would affect her ability to work. "I was seated next to an artist at an event who told me artists aren't supposed to have children because it affects their creative output and energy, and those words resounded in my head," Chapman remembers. Luckily, her experience was the exact opposite: as her pregnancy progressed, she says she felt more inspired, more compelled to create. (231)

Women have access to the ultimate "secret," the potential and experience of pregnancy. According to Bachelard (1994), "all we communicate to others is an orientation towards what is secret without ever being able to tell the secret objectively. What is secret never has total objectivity" (13).

In this section, I expand on the finding that women experience pregnancy as a secret (Sundstrom 2013) to describe how women perceive pregnancy as a secret to share and the secret knowledge of experiencing pregnancy. One participant described her experience keeping the secret:

> For whatever reason, I didn't think it had happened that month, so I was sort of in disbelief and I know that I took the pregnancy test and I almost didn't tell my husband I was going to take it, I was just double checking that I wasn't, I was sure that I wasn't, I was just double checking.

This experience explicates the link between the surprise of pregnancy and the need to keep it a secret. In U.S. culture, pregnancy generally remains a "secret" until the end of the first trimester, when it is socially acceptable to "tell" this secret to family and friends. Participants felt silenced by the need to keep their pregnancies a secret until the twelfth week. Although the risk of miscarriage drops precipitously by the second trimester, participants believed that the social norm to hide a pregnancy until the twelfth week stigmatized miscarriage. Research suggests that although up to 31% of confirmed pregnancies end in miscarriage, women experience stigma and silence around this experience (Peel 2010; Gold et al. 2012; MacGeorge and Wilkum 2012). The social norms of medicalization and control construct secrecy around the female body and pregnancy.

The act of conception takes place in secret, the biological process of conception is often referred to as a mystery, secret, or "miracle." The result of conception, however, leaves one of the agents very much in public communication with her community while the other agent remains unaffected and in secret. Sex, pregnancy, and gender converge in Hawthorne's *Scarlet Letter*, "the enigmatic meaning of secrecy lies in the potent effects the scarlet letter may have produced as a bearer of secrecy in the life histories of those affected by it" (van Manen 1996, 46). The story portrays the public shame and the private valor of the heroine, though her valor is only known to the reader (and the father of the unborn child) and remains a secret from the community that shames her.

### *The Pregnant Body*

The dichotomy of outside and inside subtly emerges in the duality of women's reproductive health. According to Bachelard (1994), "outside and inside form a dialectic of division, the obvious geometry of which blinds us as soon as we bring it into play in metaphorical domains. It has the sharpness of yes and no, which decides everything" (211). The sharpness of yes and no can be understood in the question, "am I pregnant?" There may be no other single question that demands the reconceptualization of the self and identity as profoundly as the possibility of reproducing.

For the first time in the twentieth century, "experts asked women to do new things: to follow expert advice and to bring themselves, their own pregnant bodies, to doctors for examination in advance of delivery" (Reagan 2012, 7). According to Welch, Schwartz, and Woloshin (2012), "pregnancy is not a disease, but increasingly doctors are treating it like one" (107). Participants in this study sought alternatives to traditional prenatal care, including midwifery practices, alternative birthing centers, and obstetrician/gynecologists who valued relationship-centered care. In particular, these women valued choice regarding exams and tests, which have become a routine part of traditional OB/GYN care (e.g., vaginal exams, blood work, genetic testing, glucose tests, and ultrasounds). Evidence suggests that many of these services are unlikely to benefit low-risk women and may cause harm (Rooks 1999). For example, the U.S. Preventive Task Force recommended against routine ultrasounds in low-risk pregnancies and the Cochrane Collaborative found that ultrasounds did not reduce adverse outcomes and may increase cesarean sections (Whitworth et al. 2010; Welch, Schwartz, and Woloshin 2012).

Participants resisted medical advice during pregnancy. These women made their own decisions about using prescription drugs, exercising, and imbibing. One participant described her midwife's advice to avoid alcohol and coffee during her pregnancy:

> I'm like, "well I'm European, and I know I'm not going to damage my baby if I have a glass of wine." I didn't tell her that. . . . In the second trimester, I have a glass of wine if I feel like it or a cup of coffee in the morning. So I don't drink more than that but I don't feel like I'm going to harm the baby by having that, and there's research that supports that.

In preparation for labor and delivery, many women sought a middle ground between a hospital and home birth, preferring alternative birthing centers. In particular, participants valued low rates of cesarean sections and episiotomies. Pregnant women desire shared decision making with health care providers to make complex choices from genetic testing to cord blood banking.

The "purist pregnant woman" myth highlights the false dichotomy between holistic pregnancy and the biomedical paradigm of pregnancy (Sundstrom 2013). Participants resisted the myth of the "purist pregnant woman" who becomes a vessel, giving up her body for the development of the fetus. Women believed that media, health care providers, and special interest groups, including La Leche League, exerted control over women's bodies by perpetuating the myth of an ideal pregnant woman (Sundstrom 2013). According to Kline (2011), "popular media medicalize health and illness via nearly exclusive reference to medical models without portraying the role of politics in decision making and deflecting attention away from non-medical strategies for resolution" (256).

Women negotiated complex meanings of their pregnant bodies. Some participants described the benefits of a pregnant body, including that the community is "kind" to pregnant women, letting them go first in line. One participant said, "it is lovely to be a pregnant woman. People are warm, they talk to you." Other participants struggled to make sense of the duality of their pregnant bodies. One participant described pregnancy as

> sacrificing who you've been for this person you're becoming and a lot of that happens during pregnancy like giving up yourself for the sake of the child and motherhood and you realize that you are not going to have your time back, or your body back, in the same way ever again.

Another participant problematized the romantic notion of the mother-to-be: "I didn't feel any connection to the baby, I feel like it's very abstract and I don't feel like I have love for the baby."

Women approach the question of pregnancy in myriad ways: with optimism, anticipation, dread, and fear. Acknowledging this multitude of experience, when we bring pregnancy into the policy realm, it often sharply divides and essentializes women of reproductive age. According to Reagan (2012), "the nation increasingly appeared to be most dedicated to protecting future babies through the bodies of women and much less concerned about the health of women and mothers themselves" (17). One recent example of the dichotomy of outside and inside, yes and no, is the CDC's Folic Acid Campaign. This campaign asks women, "are you able to get pregnant?" and instructs them to plan accordingly. In this way, the CDC's Folic Acid campaign is geared toward all women of reproductive age. All women of reproductive age, from first menstruation through menopause, are encouraged to take folic acid supplements each day. Pregnant women have long been advised to take folic acid, because it helps prevent neural tube disorders. If we know that folic acid prevents birth defects, what is the harm of advising women to take folic acid everyday?

The campaign purposefully avoids the fact that women can consume too much folic acid. In fact, research suggests that women who take a folic acid supplement often exceed the daily limit because many of our foods, such as breakfast cereals, are already fortified with folic acid. Too much folic acid can mask B-12 deficiency and serious health issues. Emerging research indicates that increased folic acid may be linked to certain cancers. Although the benefits may outweigh the costs among pregnant women and those planning to become pregnant, the folic acid campaign reduces women to their reproductive capability.

According to Parrott and Kreuter (2011), "health communication researchers sought to understand the effects of communicating about a role for folic acid on women's health practices" (6). The outside/inside division is evident in the target population of the campaign. Instead of targeting women who plan to become pregnant, the campaign encourages "women who are able to get pregnant" to take folic acid. Even women who are using contraception are emphatically encouraged to take folic acid because "half of all pregnancies in the United States are not planned." It seems that the logical campaign strategy to prevent neural tube defects resulting from unplanned pregnancies is to reduce unplanned pregnancies. Furthermore, this line of reasoning suggests that once a woman finds herself in a position of an unplanned pregnancy, the only option is to have a baby.

The danger of campaigns that reduce women to a biological, reproductive function is that this outside/inside, yes/no division blinds us to the fact that this campaign, which is aimed at women, is not about women's health. This campaign is not about improving women's health. This campaign is about preventing neural tube defects in *potential* fetuses. According to Roberts (1997), "feminists use the term 'maternal-fetal conflict' to describe the way in which law, social policies, and medical practice sometimes treat a pregnant woman's interests in opposition to those of the fetus she is carrying"

(40). The campaign literature tells women that they aren't smart enough to prevent pregnancy: after all, half of all pregnancies are unplanned. The campaign creates an inside/outside dichotomy of women who are able to become pregnant (or those who aren't aware of infertility) and women who are not able to become pregnant. The campaign does not consider that some women don't want to become pregnant now (or ever). In other words, only women who will become pregnant matter.

## *Pregnancy in the Digital Age*

Pregnant women spend time using traditional and new media to seek information about pregnancy and healthy behaviors (Sundstrom 2013). Almost all the pregnant women I talked with read the best-selling book *What to Expect When You're Expecting* by Heidi Murkoff. Participants uniformly downloaded mobile applications or apps to assist them with every aspect of conception, pregnancy, labor, and delivery. According to one participant who used an app to help her conceive and throughout her pregnancy:

> It was helpful, you know everything regarding pregnancy was so new to me. I didn't really have any close family members or really any close friends who were pregnant or had a baby really in any kind of close time frame around when I was trying to get pregnant. Then I found an app that was helpful because one it was confidential and two it just made everything really easy and clear so I really liked it.

Popular apps included babycenter.com and babybumpapp.com

These women also signed up for Text4baby, a free text-messaging program, which provides prenatal and post-partum health and safety information to over 740,000 pregnant women across the United States. Text4baby is led by the National Healthy Mothers, Healthy Babies Coalition (HMHB) in partnership with a broad, public-private collaboration that includes government, non-profit organizations, academic institutions, professional associations, tribal agencies, and corporations. Women sign up by texting BABY (or BEBE for Spanish messages) to 511411. Launched in February 2010, Text4baby is the first national mobile health initiative in the United States.

When registering for Text4baby, women enter the due date or baby's date of birth to receive timely messages. Women receive a standard series of start-up health messages, followed by messages during pregnancy and the first 12 months of their baby's life. The messages cover a range of topics including health care access, prenatal care, influenza, nutrition, mental health, labor and delivery, and car seat safety. For example, a message around 12 weeks of pregnancy informs women, "Your baby is growing a lot! Baby is now the size of a lime & can open its mouth & move its tiny hands."

Women appreciated Text4baby's tailored information based on due date. Timely reminders, such as scheduling doctor's appointments, were particularly well received among participants. Some women described opting out due to too many text messages. Other women believed that additional tailoring of messages based on an individual's needs would improve the service. In a related study, my co-author and I found that the Text4baby campaign would be most effective if women could text questions to receive personal answers to their health and pregnancy questions (Briones and Sundstrom 2013).

In addition to mobile apps and texting, women visited online communities to find more information about pregnancy. One participant reported,

> I read blogs by other moms and a lot of those will address the life of being a mom because some of them aren't necessarily pregnant at the times they're writing so I guess kind of connecting with women who have gone through it before and what their suggestions are.

These women valued the expertise of women who had experienced pregnancy and sought answers to their health questions online in community forums and blogs.

## CONCLUSION

This chapter deconstructs issues of identity, power, and body politics by (re)writing the body. This chapter explicates the body politic of pregnancy and offers an understanding of how medicalization has impacted women's experience of pregnancy. This analysis answers the questions: (1) How do women make meaning of the physiological experience of pregnancy?; (2) How do women make meaning of the medical experiences they have encountered during pregnancy?; and (3) How do women make meaning of campaigns and messages addressing pregnancy, from preconception care to home births?

In order to reconnect the self and the body, we must understand the critical disconnect between our bodies and ourselves. These stories of pregnancy uncover the medicalization that creates distance between the self and the body. Perhaps we can come to know and understand the body in a cultural and historical sense by deconstructing the political, patriarchal system that seeks to wrest our bodies out of our control. Traditionally, women served as keepers of the secrets of healing and bodily knowledge. When health and bodies were the domain of the domestic sphere, women exerted more control over bodily knowledge and history. Perhaps we can find and share this knowledge that has been lost by uncovering the political system that devalues women and seeks to limit their agency and control their bodies.

Perhaps we can come to know our bodies again by constructing new knowledge through listening to and trusting women.

## *Chapter Three*

# Childbirth

## *The Intersection of Maternal and Child Health*

Birth centers and home births offer women an alternative to delivering in a hospital. According to the Cochrane Collaboration, hospital births often lead to increased interventions and complications without any improvement in safety compared to planned home births assisted by qualified midwives (Olsen and Clausen 1996). Home births, which still account for less than 1% of all births in the United States, increased by 29% between 2004 and 2009 (MacDorman, Mathews, and Declercq 2012). In the previous chapter, pregnant women described the need for alternative birthing options to meet their needs in labor and delivery. Despite growing need and interest in birth centers and midwifery, laws and regulations continue to limit women's choices in childbirth. The American College of Obstetricians and Gynecologists (ACOG) opposes planned home births and does not support midwives who are not certified by the American College of Nurse-Midwives or the American Midwifery Certification Board (American College of Obstetricians and Gynecologists 2013).

Labor and delivery is an area of women's reproductive health receiving increased national attention. Many states continue to increase restrictions on midwives and birthing centers. In South Carolina, the S.C. Department of Health and Environmental Control threatened to close birth centers twice in less than one year based on a state regulation requiring birth centers to maintain an on-call physician. This (re)interpretation of the 1975 state regulation led to rallies, letters to DHEC, and calls to Governor Haley's office from supporters of natural birth. The American Association of Birth Centers, the Commission for the Accreditation of Birth Centers, and the American College of Nurse-Midwives wrote letters to DHEC in opposition to the interpretation. Experts argued that this requirement would cause unnecessary delays and disrupt timely, appropriate transfers to hospitals in emergency situations. Stakeholders are currently attempting to update the law with a bill that would remove the on-call physician requirement, instead requiring that birth centers maintain hospital transfer guidelines for emergencies, as well as meet the American Association of Birth Centers accreditation standards.

Following the previous discussion of pregnancy and expectations of labor and delivery, this chapter describes the experience of childbirth. I present findings from 44 in-depth interviews with biological mothers of newborns in the immediate post-partum period. All interviews were conducted within two weeks of the birth of an infant, many in the hospital maternity ward. Among participants, although each experience was unique, listening to and understanding these women's birth stories created a unique rapport between researcher and participant. This chapter explores (1) the physiological experience of childbirth, (2) perceptions of medicine and the biomedical model surrounding childbirth, and (3) perceptions of mediated messages about childbirth. Participants' birth stories offered an in-depth understanding of their values, their relationship with their doctor, and their beliefs regarding the medical model.

The first known use of the term birth emerged in the thirteenth century, derived from Middle English and originally of Scandinavian origin, meaning "the emergence and separation of offspring from the body of the mother" (The American Heritage Dictionary 2014). In this definition, the agency of the mother is absent and only the body of the mother is required for birth. The evolution of the term birth is evidenced in the definition "to produce, originate, or create" (Collins English Dictionary 2003). An expanded meaning of birth includes "the act or process of bearing young" and "to deliver (a baby)" (The American Heritage Dictionary 2014).

The first known use of delivery as "the act or process of giving birth" emerged in the fifteenth century (Merriam-Webster 2004). Delivery derives from the late Latin *deliberare* and Latin *liberare* meaning "to set free." In other words, delivery is to liberate, save, or hand over. Delivery is also defined as "the procedure of assisting the birth of the fetus and expulsion of the placenta by manual, instrumental, or surgical means" (Merriam-Webster 2004). This definition introduces a third party and renders the mother invisible. Parturition, a medical synonym for delivery, is "the action or process of giving birth to offspring" (Merriam-Webster 2004). The first known use of parturition was in 1646 and emerged from the late Latin *parturition-*, *parturitio,* and from Latin *parturire.* Although delivery and parturition allude to an active subject "giving birth," they also privilege a biomedical interpretation of delivery that necessitates assistance.

In contrast to medicalized definitions of delivery and birth, in which the laboring woman is noticeably absent, the term midwife, derived from Middle

English *midwyf* means "with-woman" or "the woman with (the mother at birth), the woman assisting" (Merriam-Webster 2004). The definition of midwife privileges the mother as an active agent during labor and delivery. In a review of historical maternal mortality rates, Loudon (2000) found that home births with trained midwives were safer than hospital deliveries by physicians. According to Rooks (1999), "whenever and wherever midwifery declined, the incidence of maternal mortality and infant deaths from birth injuries increased" (30).

In the 1800s, doctors competed with midwives for the business of labor and delivery. According to Ehrenreich and English (2010),

> the suppression of women health workers and the rise to dominance of male professionals was not a "natural" process, resulting automatically from changes in medical science, nor was it the result of women's failure to take on health work. It was an active takeover by male professionals. (4)

In the late nineteenth century, "various solutions to 'the midwife problem' were proposed. Private practitioners and academic obstetricians wanted midwives to be brought under the control of doctors and to eliminate them as soon as possible" (Rooks 1999, 26).

According to Pollock (1999), early doctors were regarded as mechanics: "the obstetrician (even in his early incarnations as male midwife and barber-surgeon) relied on women for his livelihood and women relied on the talismanic charm of medical instruments" (14). Without the training and experience of midwives, doctors competed for patients with risky obstetric tools, such as forceps, episiotomy, anesthesia, and cesarean section (Wolf 2011). According to Leavitt (1997), "physicians could not come into the birthing room and do nothing. One Kansas doctor admitted, 'Perhaps the best way to manage normal labor is to let it alone, but you cannot hold down a job and do that'" (46). Obstetricians at this time lacked a basic understanding of germ theory, frequently completing autopsies and attending childbirth without washing their hands. Ignaz Semmelweis showed that doctors could prevent puerperal fever by using antisepsis, however, it took more than twenty years for this practice to be widely adopted (Loudon 2000).

Scholars have uncovered the historical, social, and cultural impact of the medicalization of childbirth in the United States (Davis-Floyd 2003; Pollock 1999; Wolf 2011). While almost all U.S. births in 1900 occurred at home, by 1969 only 1% of births took place at home (MacDorman, Mathews, and Declercq 2012). Through 1937, maternal mortality rates were highest among upper-class women, most likely because they could afford a physician and the accompanied unwarranted surgical interference, while poor women were treated by trained midwives (Loudon 2000). According to Pollock (1999), the increase of hospital births in the twentieth century fundamentally changed the social rite of birth:

> The ideal of a safe birth had its costs, among them the collapse of women's birthing culture and the power that culture secured for women as women. . . . It sacrificed the rich social history that brought women together in the birthing room—often across family and community lines—to the efficiency and sterility of the hospital ward. Routinely isolated, drugged, and often physically restrained, the woman giving birth in a hospital in the early part of the twentieth century was literally cut off from all social resources. She was not only physically but socially debilitated. As a result, her agency was easily usurped by the attending physicians. (12)

Women's fear of labor pain and anxiety about birth led to the acceptance of epidural anesthesia and other interventions, including cesarean section (Wolf 2011). According to Rooks (1999),

> medicine strengthened its role in maternity care by expanding the concept of obstetric pathology, using hypersensitive monitoring devices, creating constrained definitions of normal, defining variation from those definitions as pathologic, and routinizing and eventually "normalizing" childbirth characterized by a sequence of preemptive interventions. (5)

The hospital birth marginalized women's lived bodily experiences by privileging medical authority. According to Leavitt (1997), "birth in the hospital encouraged interference because the equipment and staff were readily accessible, and this interference increased the number of maternal deaths" (50). The normalcy of hospital birth is supported by media, physicians, prenatal classes, and women's fears and desires for a safe birth. Even women's own birth stories

> may be complicitous with the system they often otherwise reject: they may convey the same threats and promises that finally moved at least one of the mothers I talked with to concede that a c-section she had vigorously opposed "could've been good." Directly and indirectly, they may support the norms—the desires and expectations for a "normal" birth—enforced by medical practice. (Pollock 1999)

For almost sixty years, a "normal" labor and delivery has been defined by Friedman's curve, which describes the length of time 500 first-time mothers giving birth in 1954 required to dilate during labor (Friedman 1955). Using this obsolete measurement may lead to increased diagnosis of "failure to progress" and more interventions, including cesarean sections (Pollock 1999; Boyle, Reddy, and Landy 2013).

While prenatal classes, especially hospital-based courses, may attempt to quell opposition from women by indoctrinating scientific and hospital norms, women use various mechanisms to reclaim "maternal identity" and resist the "unquestioned authority of medical science" (Pollock 1999). According to Martin (2001),

> women themselves may try to reduce the amount of time they spend in the hospital by delaying admitting themselves as long as possible. Explicitly they often understand that this allows a shorter time for their labors to be defined as ineffective and their baby to be extracted operatively. (141)

Davis-Floyd (2003) described the holistic paradigm as an alternative to biomedical or technocratic birth and introduced a humanistic approach to birth. Humanistic care may include hospital births and various interventions rejected by holistic care, however, a humanist ideology emphasizes a relational approach to birth and medical care (Davis-Floyd 2003). This approach rejects the pathologizing of birth, including

> frequent use of methods to induce labor and make women labor harder and faster; withholding food and drink from women who are working hard (i.e., in "labor") in case they might need cesarean sections; rupturing the bag of fluid surrounding the baby in order to "speed things up" and to make it possible to attach electrodes to the baby's head; and cutting women's vaginas and perineums on a routine basis. (Rooks 1999, 127–128)

One global attempt to promote humanistic care includes the Baby-Friendly Hospital Initiative (BFHI) sponsored by the World Health Organization (WHO) and the United Nations Children's Fund (UNICEF). The BFHI officially designates hospitals and birthing centers that support breastfeeding and mother-infant bonding. Hospitals receive special recognition when they offer mothers the information, confidence, and skills to successfully initiate and continue breastfeeding (www.babyfriendlyusa.org). A "Baby-Friendly" hospital implements ten steps to protect and promote breastfeeding and must not accept free or low-cost formula giveaways. More than 15,000 facilities in 134 countries have been awarded "Baby-Friendly" status leading to more mothers breastfeeding their infants and improving child health.

## BIRTH STORIES IN RHODE ISLAND

As the nation's smallest state, 73% of all births in Rhode Island take place at one hospital. In 2011, Rhode Island became the first state to stop formula giveaways at all seven birthing hospitals. According to the 2010 census, Rhode Island had 544,167 female residents, which comprised 51.7% of Rhode Island's population. Forty percent of women in Rhode Island are of childbearing age, between 15 and 44 years (U.S. Census Bureau 2010a). Fewer than half of households in Rhode Island (44%) consist of a husband-wife pair and 13.5% of families are female head of household. While 17% of households include a husband-wife pair with children under 18, female head of household with a child under eighteen years of age accounts for 7.7% of all households. Almost 9% of households are females under 65 living alone (U. S. Census Bureau 2010b).

In 2008, there were 12,048 births in Rhode Island and the birth rate was 11.5 births per 1,000, slightly below the national average. Almost 50% of infants were born to white mothers, 21.6% born to Latina mothers, 8.4% to black mothers, and 4.3% to Asian mothers. Although Rhode Island's racial and ethnic breakdown is approximately 76% white, 12% Latina, 5% black, 3% Asian, 3% two or more races, and 0.6% Native American (U.S. Census Bureau 2010b), birth rate trends in Rhode Island mirror national data with Latina and black birth rates outpacing white birth rates (Kaiser Family Foundation 2008a).

Preterm births and cesarean delivery rates vary by race/ethnicity in Rhode Island. In 2008, 11.2% of all births were preterm births (national average 12.3%), with the black and Latina preterm birth rates higher than those for white women in Rhode Island. Thirty-three percent of births were by cesarean delivery. White women (36.2%) had the highest rates of cesarean delivery while Latina women (27.9%) had the lowest (Kaiser Family Foundation 2008b). Women in Rhode Island face barriers to health care. Although 84.5% of women in Rhode Island received prenatal care in the first trimester of pregnancy in 2008, only 75.7% of Latina women and 74.2% of black women began prenatal care in the first trimester compared with 90% of white women (Kaiser Family Foundation 2006).

### *Birth Narratives*

I talked with women on the hospital maternity inpatient wards at one hospital in Rhode Island. All biological mothers who experienced a live birth at the Hospital during the study enrollment period of January 10, 2012 through January 27, 2012 were considered eligible for the study. I worked closely with nursing staff to ensure that I respected the hospital setting in which my research was conducted. If the nurses were uncomfortable that a family was in a crisis and would be upset, I respected that concern and did not approach the mother. I worked with the nursing staff to determine this on a case-by-case basis. I also talked with the nursing staff to identify what issues led to them feeling that it was not appropriate for families to be contacted. On a number of occasions, nurses requested that I did not approach certain patients because they needed to rest for health reasons, they had an emotional visit with a social worker, or they were simply overwhelmed.

In addition to talking with the nursing staff, research staff used the hospital's computer system to pre-determine eligibility. Mothers had to be able to communicate in English to participate in the study. Formal exclusion criteria included: (1) the mother not living in Rhode Island at the time of the child's birth, (2) cognitive impairment that prevents obtaining consent and answering the study questions, (3) maternal age less than 18 years, (4) serious illness of the newborn such that it would be upsetting to contact the mother, and (5) the family is already participating in three or more studies so that an additional study would be a burden. In addition to the formal exclusion criteria, mothers were not approached if the mother or child was seriously ill. Mothers were also not approached if the child was in DCYF custody or under a DCYF hold, as again this was a family crisis, as well as having the further complication of the mother possibly not having parental responsibility. The most common reasons for participants' ineligibility were inability to speak English, state of residence (outside of Rhode Island), and mother's health.

The Division of Research loaned me a white coat worn by all physicians and researchers in the hospital. I wrote a number of memos about the impact of the white coat on the researcher-researched relationship and the power imbalance it created. The white coat symbolically allowed me entrance to the hospital and the patients' rooms. Research indicates that the white coat is a strong non-verbal communication device, which evokes confidence, trust, and empathy toward the wearer (Chung et al. 2012). A recent study suggested that wearing the white coat not only exerts power over others, this article of clothing impacts the psychological and behavioral processes of the wearer. Adam and Galinsky (2012) found that the symbolic meaning of the white coat and the physical experience of wearing it influenced how individuals thought, felt, and acted. This research offered an "enclothed cognition" perspective, in which individuals wearing the doctor's white coat completed tasks with more attention than others (Adam and Galinsky 2012).

I began enrolling study participants on January 11, after IRB approval was obtained, and continued enrollment until January 27. I recruited and consented all participants in person at the hospital and conducted all interviews either in person or over the telephone. Interviewing continued until February 12, when a point of theoretical saturation had been achieved, which included 44 women. Of the 44 in-depth interviews, 27 took place at the hospital and 17 took place over the telephone. In all, I spent 19 days at the hospital and a total of 157 hours or a little more than eight hours per day "on site." The interviews averaged one hour in length.

Ideally, I would have conducted all in-person interviews with mothers of newborns in a protected place and at a protected time. However, it was important to recognize that some mothers of newborns may be particularly fatigued and some women had visitors and hospital personnel coming in and out of their hospital room. By offering two options to complete the study, I deferred to the participants' preference. Furthermore, I found that "a phone interview can be as intimate and engrossing, and ultimately just as good at getting full responses, as an in-person interview" (Lindlof and Taylor 2010, 190). In addition, phone interviews allowed participants to speak more freely because they had a greater sense of anonymity.

Mothers who preferred a telephone interview were asked to schedule a date and time for the interview within one week of discharge. I called participants one day prior to the interview as a reminder. The interview protocol for the telephone interview was the same as the interview protocol for the in-person interview at the hospital. All participants were informed of the researcher's wish to audiotape the interview for purposes of accuracy. After obtaining informed consent, the mothers were interviewed. Participants received a $25 gift card to compensate them for their time and efforts in the study.

Overall, 304 patients were reviewed with 248 (81.6%) screened as eligible for inclusion in the study and 56 (18.4%) deemed ineligible for participation. Of the 248 eligible participants, 120 were not approached as they were discharged prior to my being able to approach them. There were many reasons that I may have missed potential participants. First, during their stay in the hospital, participants were not always eligible or available for the study due to maternal or infant health. Many mothers posted a "resting: please do not disturb" sign on their door for most of the day. The best time to talk with participants was during the morning, so I often arrived on the floors before 9 a.m. Afternoons in the hospital were busy and interviews were often delayed by visits from nurses, OBs, pediatricians, midwives, lactation consultants, social workers, anesthesiologists, birth certificate procedures, baby's first photo, nutrition services, and housekeeping. Some of these "delays" led to the best interviews, because they built a strong rapport with the participant. I attempted to vary my time on each of the floors, so that I was on each floor at a different time of day, however, by the time I made it back to some of the floors, potential participants had already been discharged. The duration of hospital stay varied greatly among participants.

Seventy-one mothers of newborns refused participation. Fifty-seven (44.5% of those approached) consented to interviews. Ultimately, 44 mothers of newborns (34.4% of those approached) participated in the study. Of those interviewed, 20 (45%) delivered by cesarean section and 24 (55%) delivered vaginally. Participants ranged from 18 to 40 years of age with an average of 29 years of age. Participants ranged from new mothers delivering their first child to the mothers of four children with an average of 1.77 children per woman.

The race/ethnicity of the participants coincided with the state's overall demographics. Of those interviewed, 28 (63.6%) identified as white, 11 (25%) identified as Latina, three (6.8%) identified as black, and 2 (4.5%)

identified as Asian. Educational attainment varied among participants as well. Only 6 participants (14%) attained more than a four-year college degree, 13 (30%) earned a four-year degree, 9 (20%) had an associate's degree or "some college," 9 (20%) earned a high school diploma, while 7 participants (16%) had less than a high school diploma. Participants are identified with a pseudonym linked to their biographical profile in table 3.1.

Many women I talked with described the experience of labor and delivery. The recent birth experience served as a major health event in their lives. Although each experience was unique, listening to and understanding participants' birth stories created a unique rapport between researcher and participant. Pseudonyms are provided to protect participants' anonymity. *Healthy People 2020* provides evidence-based, national benchmarks to improve the health and well-being of women, infants, children, and families. The Maternal, Infant, and Child Health objectives include reducing maternal morbidity and mortality, fetal and infant deaths, low birth weight and preterm births, and cesarean births among low-risk (full-term, singleton, and vertex presentation) women. A review of the Agency for Healthcare Research and Quality (AHRQ) future research needs projects in topics related to women's health suggests that priority future research needs involve improving risk communication and decision making in childbirth (Cottrell et al. 2012; Lewis et al. 2012).

Destiny is 29 years old (Latina). She has three children and completed the ninth grade. She described an unexpected breech presentation at delivery and her desire to avoid a cesarean delivery:

> It was a very different experience from having my other two kids. He was breech and the doctor didn't know that. I never delivered a breech baby before. They wanted to do an emergency c-section. I really didn't want to have a c-section. I just wish that they had done an ultrasound to see what position the baby was in. I told them that he's not moving a lot, he wasn't moving a lot at the end, like the other two.
>
> They did do a stress test, but I felt that they didn't do everything they could to see if he was breech. The doctor, I think she was embarrassed that she didn't deliver a breech baby before. It was scary. She said, "I'm just going to let her try to push a couple more times." I mean, he was half way out already, and then they say, now I need a c-section? I wasn't going to do it. It was really scary for me and for him too, I think. I didn't know what was happening. I was so scared. When he came out, I heard him crying, and I knew everything was okay with him. It was a very dramatic experience.
>
> I hope that the Doctor, she can learn from this experience and not let it happen to anyone else. I was hoping she would come up to the room to see me [after the birth]. But she never did come up to the room. (Destiny)

As in Destiny's birth story, women express dissatisfaction with childbirth when they perceive it as something happening to them (Fisher et al. 2012). In order to improve women's birth outcomes and childbirth experiences, scholars suggest that understanding women's beliefs and attitudes is crucial to providing woman-centered care (Haines et al. 2012). In a recent study, women described the need for more information and increased control of the childbirth experience (Koehn 2008). At the same time, fewer women are attending childbirth education classes, which traditionally provided education and information about labor and delivery (Morton and Hsu 2007). Studies show that women's satisfaction with the birth experience is strongly related to involvement in decision making and ability to exercise choice and control (Cook and Loomis 2012; Dencker et al. 2010).

Lilly is 26 years old (white). She completed college. She described her plan for a natural childbirth and the resulting cesarean delivery with her first child:

> I had a 40-hour labor. I ended up having a c-section. But, she makes it all worth it. We came in around midnight on Friday. My labor was progressing very slowly. I wanted a natural childbirth. I had a birth plan and my doctor had "okayed" it. By 7 a.m., I was still not dilating. They said they wanted to give me Pitocin, which I was very upset about. So, the doctor said we could wait. So, we waited.
>
> By 6am on Saturday, I had an infection and a 101 degree temperature. I felt defeated. They said I was so tired and sick that I really needed an epidural. So, I got an epidural and I ended up with Pitocin, after all. I pushed for an hour and a half. The epidural was wearing off. My doctor was really amazing, she just kept saying, "I want you guys to do what you feel." She gave us the option to push for another hour. So, I pushed for another hour. Then, I just felt so defeated. So, I ended up with a c-section.
>
> She was born on Sunday at 2 a.m. She was 8 lbs 12 ounces. She was healthy. My infection didn't affect her. I was exhausted and had a temperature of 103. It was a very amazing experience. I feel like I had everything happen to me. I got to have a natural labor. I got to have an epidural. When the epidural wore off, I got to push naturally. And then I had a c-section. It was very emotional. But the care here has been wonderful. (Lilly)

Lilly's birth story follows a common progression of labor augmentation, epidural analgesia, and cesarean delivery. Labor management decisions impact the probability of cesarean delivery. Interventions that may increase the potential for cesarean delivery include labor induction, labor neuroaxial anesthesia, operative vaginal delivery, and evaluation of fetal factors (Spong et al. 2012). Research demonstrates that continuous fetal heart rate monitoring causes unnecessary interventions, including increased cesarean deliveries, which results in a rise in morbidity and mortality among women (Spong et al. 2012; Romano and Lothian 2008).

The number of cesarean deliveries has risen dramatically since 1990, however, higher rates have not improved birth outcomes (Gould et al. 2004).

Cesarean delivery increases the risk of maternal health problems, such as intraoperative complications, and impacts future deliveries (Spong et al. 2012). The results of cesarean delivery, including adhesions, abnormal placentation, and uterine rupture, pose serious health risks for mother and newborn (Clark and Smith 2011). A national cesarean delivery rate over 30% imposes a significant burden on the health and well-being of women and infants, as well as the health care system (Spong et al. 2012).

In March 2014, the American College of Obstetricians and Gynecologists (ACOG) and the Society for Maternal-Fetal Medicine (SMFM) issued a consensus statement on the safe prevention of the primary cesarean delivery. The joint statement indicates the need to prevent unnecessary cesareans among nulliparous women. As of January 1, 2014, the Joint Commission requires hospitals with 1,100 or more births per year to include the perinatal care measure set as the mandatory fifth measure set. The performance measurement requirements aim to decrease the rate of nulliparous women with a full-term, singleton baby in a vertex position delivered by cesarean section (Zhani 2012). The Healthy People guidelines aim to reduce cesarean birth among low-risk women with no prior cesarean birth to 23.9% by 2020 (HealthyPeople.gov 2014).

In 2012, the Eunice Kennedy Shriver National Institute of Child Health and Human Development, the Society for Maternal-Fetal Medicine, and the American College of Obstetricians and Gynecologists hosted a joint workshop to develop solutions for "preventing the first cesarean delivery" (Spong et al. 2012). In addition, the World Health Organization, Lamaze International, Coalition for Improving Maternity Services, and Childbirth Connection, among a host of other groups, are also working to reduce the number of cesarean deliveries.

Research suggests that women with unplanned cesarean deliveries are less satisfied with childbirth compared with women who experienced vaginal delivery (Malacrida and Boulton 2012). One of the top three future needs as prioritized by AHRQ stakeholders in understanding Vaginal Birth After Cesarean (VBAC) included understanding how patients perceive risk and how best to communicate risks (Cottrell et al. 2012). In order to reduce the rate of cesarean birth among low-risk women, researchers need to better understand the role of informed medical decision making (Lewis et al. 2012). Extant literature indicates that empowering women to take control of labor and delivery by making informed choices through shared decision making will lead to better birth outcomes (Koehn 2008; Cook and Loomis 2012; Dencker et al. 2010).

Participants described the consequences of the medical establishment ignoring their requests for tests or treatment. One participant discussed choosing a new OB/GYN practice and demanding a c-section for her newborn as a result of her last delivery. Emma is 26 years old (white). She has three children and completed high school. After a prior traumatic delivery, Emma demanded a cesarean delivery:

> When I was pregnant with my daughter in 2006, I thought she would be big, because my son was 8 pounds, 11 ounces. So I wanted them to do an ultrasound to find out how big she was. They hadn't done an ultrasound for weeks. I was really worried about it. And during delivery, she ended up getting shoulder dystocia. The nurses were pushing on my stomach to get her out. It was really scary. She ended up being 9 pounds, 11 ounces. She was in the NICU. So, I demanded a c-section for this pregnancy. And she ended up being a peanut, 6 pounds, 13 ounces. (Emma)

As Emma's story demonstrates, women negotiate complex understandings of cesarean delivery and important outcomes may be influenced by prior experiences and understandings of risk. Nonmedically indicated cesarean delivery may be impacted by patient perception and education, social norms, and social media (Spong et al. 2012).

Scholars suggest that improving women's satisfaction with childbirth requires empowering women with information, including the risks and benefits of interventions, and decision making tools to make informed choices (Fisher et al. 2012; Hidaka and Callister 2012). Although many health care providers dismiss the birth plan as outdated, scholars argue that women and couples benefit from identifying their needs and preferences, accessing resources, and improving patient-provider communication through the development of a birth plan (Kaufman 2007). Spong and colleagues (2012) suggest that health care provider type (e.g., physician, certified nurse midwife) may be related to labor outcomes.

According to Davis-Floyd (2004), women may feel coerced by hospital staff to accept an epidural. Abigail is 26 years old and white. She has three children. She completed the eleventh grade and earned her GED. She described receiving an epidural, despite an all-natural birth plan and a fear of needles:

> I planned to have an all-natural delivery in the Alternative Birthing Center (ABC). My first birth was all-natural. My second birth, I had really bad contractions, I went to the hospital and my placenta was detaching, so they prepped me for an emergency c-section. But, they gave me an epidural and he came right out. I said, "I have to push." They told me "no, you don't." I said, "yes, I have to push." And he came out.
>
> I have a great fear of needles. Everyone says that one needle doesn't compare with the pain of delivery. But I am skeeved out at thoughts about needles. The needle causes more stress than labor and delivery. With this labor and delivery, I was at home for an hour with pains. They were really gapped. I kept remembering what my doctor said, "5-1-1." I said, "I am just going to go to the Doctor. I didn't listen to the 5-1-1 rule." And when I got there, to the

> hospital, I was 4 centimeters dilated. And my contractions were 1 minute apart, and then 30 seconds apart.
>
> The nurse said, "you're going to have this baby right now. You need to make a decision about the ABC right now." And they said, "if you want medication or if you want an epidural, you can't go to the ABC." And the pain was worse than I remembered it. So, I thought, "I don't know now!" I didn't know how long it was going to be.
>
> But, this labor was so different. The others took forever. With this one, they gave me an epidural and she just came out. They literally just finished giving me the epidural. They told me that it was going to kick-in in about 15 minutes. "So, just relax." But, as soon as they said that, my water broke.
>
> I hate needles. As soon as I said I wanted the epidural, I could feel my body tensing. My neck muscles hurt. It felt longer waiting for the needle than delivering the baby. I was breathing to calm myself.
>
> She came right out: As soon as they finished giving me the epidural. My legs went numb about 15 minutes after pushing her out. I had the epidural and my water broke. The nurse said there was some meconium. The doctor wasn't even in the room.
>
> The nurse yelled, "she's coming out! Stop pushing!" I said, "I'm not! I can't help it."
>
> She just came out. The doctor couldn't believe it happened the way it did. She came flying out. It was such an unexpected experience. It was good because it was so quick.
>
> I was sitting up and she was coming out. It was a good experience. It was more pain to get the epidural. You don't know the future. If I could have seen. . . . I would have just gone ahead with the natural birth. (Abigail)

Hospital births are likely to include medical interventions, with 22% of these births including labor induction, such as Pitocin, and 63% involving epidural analgesia (Lyerly et al. 2009). The probability of vaginal delivery is lower after labor induction compared with spontaneous labor (Spong et al. 2012). The World Health Organization identified evidence-based care practices that support physiological birth, which include avoiding medically unnecessary labor induction, allowing freedom of movement during labor, providing continuous labor support, and avoiding routine interventions (Romano and Lothian 2008). Studies suggest that women lack information about the physiological process of birth and the risks of routine interventions, such as intravenous fluids, continuous electronic fetal monitoring, elective induction, epidurals and other pain medication, episiotomies, and cesarean delivery, among others (Fisher et al. 2012; Hidaka and Callister 2012).

Extant research indicates that interventions during childbirth, such as labor augmentation and unplanned cesarean delivery, may lead to maternal dissatisfaction (Dencker et al. 2010). Studies show that women often lack adequate information about the harms and benefits of routine obstetrical interventions and that increasing knowledge of their options during labor and delivery would improve their ability to make their own decisions (Koehn

2008). Informed choice during labor and delivery is fundamental to supporting women's psychosocial well-being (Haines et al. 2012).

## PERCEPTIONS OF MEDIA

Research indicates that growing numbers of pregnant women use the Internet and social media to seek information about childbirth (Romano 2007; Romano, Gerber, and Andrews 2010). However, a gap exists in our understanding of how and why women use these channels (Song et al. 2012). The women I talked with used Facebook to seek support regarding health topics. They described Facebook as a place to seek social and emotional support. Gia, a 35-year-old (white) first-time mother who had completed college, offered a particularly poignant story of using Facebook as motivation through labor and delivery:

> We actually used Facebook during labor. I hadn't slept since Saturday morning. On Monday, Tom went on Facebook and told everyone what was going on and said, "Gia needs support." That was one of the first times we had used Facebook to try and get support to cheer us on. So when I was grumpy on Monday night, he read people's encouragement to me and knowing that everyone was wishing us well and hoping for us and can't wait to meet her and all that. To me, that's more of what Facebook is for, than saying "I went to the ballpark" or "I'm chewing gum." It's funny because my husband said this morning, there were so many nice comments and people asking for updates and now that we are through it, they've already moved on to something else. But what about Gia? We're no longer the hot topic. It's all over. I'm good, she's good, and Facebook has moved on. (Gia)

These women described pregnancy as a time when they tried new media platforms. According to Kaylee, a 36-year-old (white) mother of two with a college education, "the first app I ever used was an ovulation app. Which it worked, we were pregnant the following month. . . . In the hospital, we also had contraction apps. The doctor was like—can you stop with the phone?" (Kaylee).

On television, these women heard about childbirth on news programs, such as the TODAY show and msnbc, as well as reality television shows, such as *One Born Every Minute* and *I Didn't Know I was Pregnant.* A culture of fear emerged around childbirth that these women resisted. In particular, participants described the role of fear in television programming while they were pregnant. According to Sophia, a 21-year-old (Latina) mother of two with a high school education,

> during my first pregnancy, I would sit and watch a lot of TV, especially pregnancy stories. You see a lot of complications through the television. It

> made me very frightened. I think you need to be careful what you watch, so you don't think that what you see is what is going to happen to you. I try not to watch too much TV, especially reality shows, like *A Baby Story* or *I Didn't Know I Was Pregnant*. Even though it is about women and what they go through, their labor and delivery, it gives fear to you, and of course you don't want that. (Sophia)

Savannah, a 29-year-old (white) first-time mother currently in graduate school, said, "there are some interesting shows, like *One Born Every Minute*, it's a real-life hospital. That scares you. I'm not sure if that is the best place to get information" (Savannah).

*One Born Every Minute* is a Lifetime docu-drama narrated by Jamie Lee Curtis about the maternity ward at Riverside Methodist Hospital in Columbus, Ohio. *I Didn't Know I Was Pregnant*, by Discovery Health, dramatizes the real-life experiences of women who didn't know they were pregnant. For example, women go to the hospital with what they believe is back pain from doing yard work or a severe case of food poisoning and are informed by hospital staff that they are in labor. Other women, who may have gained as little as seven pounds during pregnancy, give birth on a boat, at an amusement park, or at home alone. Some women describe suspecting pregnancy early on and taking multiple negative pregnancy tests. Many women believe they aren't pregnant because they use contraception and continue bleeding during pregnancy, which they misinterpret as menstruation.

## CONCLUSION

The loss of the right to control your body leads to the loss of economic independence, the loss of power in relationships, and ultimately the loss of freedom. According to Leavitt (1997),

> the physical removal of childbirth from the women's home to the physician's institution shifted the balance of power. Birth was no longer part of the woman's domain, as it had been during all the years it remained in the home. It had become instead a medical affair run by medical professionals. Women were no longer the main actors, but instead physicians acted upon women's bodies. (52)

Denying women's reproductive justice in childbirth perpetuates cycles of oppression and discrimination. We see these consequences when women are fired because of a pregnancy, denied maternity leave, and when statistics show that mothers make less money than women without children. The metaphor of a "closed door" illustrates women's varied reproductive experiences. The breeze from a door slamming shut exemplifies young women's experiences with education as girl's bodies remain absent from learning (Satina and

Aaliyah is 25 years old, black. She has three children. She completed some high school.

Abigail is 26 years old, black. She has three children. She completed the 11th grade and earned her GED.

Addison is 40 years old, white. She has three children. She completed college.

Adriana is 22 years old, white. She has one child. She completed college.

Alexa is 34 years old, white. She has two children. She has a PhD.

Allison is 31 years old, white. She has one child. She is a physician.

Alyssa is 26 years old, white. She has one child. She completed high school and is pursuing an Associate's degree.

Amaya is 29 years old, Latina. She has two children. She completed high school.

Amelia is 27 years old, Asian. She has one child. She completed college.

Ariana is 29 years old, white. She has one child. She completed college.

Aubrey is 25 years old, Latina. She has two children. She had her first child at the age of 17. She completed high school.

Autumn is 29 years old, white. She has two children. She completed some college.

Ava is 34 years old, Latina. She has two children. She completed some college.

Camila is 27 years old, white. She has one child. She completed some college.

Caroline is 26 years old, white. She has one child. She completed college.

Destiny is 29 years old, Latina. She has three children. She completed the ninth grade.

Emma is 26 years old, white. She has three children. She completed high school.

Faith is 40 years old, white. She has four children. She completed some college.

Gia is 35 years old, white. She has one child. She completed college.

Gianna is 19 years old, white. She has one child. She has completed some college.

Giuliana is 24 years old, Latina. She has one child. She completed high school.

Hannah is 22 years old, Latina. She has four children. She completed the 10th grade.

Isabella is 39 years old, white. She has one child. She completed college.

Isla is 35 years old, white. She has one child. She completed college.

**Table 3.1**

Hultgren 2001). When women seek to avoid shutting the door on their future plans, they may face the closed door of the clinic, where they access contraception or abortion. Although women spend most of their reproductive years

| |
|---|
| Jasmine is 32 years old, Latina. She has two children. She completed high school. |
| Kaylee is 36 years old, white. She has two children. She completed college. |
| Khloe is 38 years old, white. She has two children. She completed college. |
| Lilly is 26 years old, white. She has one child. She completed college. |
| Mackenzie is 23 years old, white. She has one child. She has completed some college. |
| Madeline is 30 years old, white. She has two children. She has completed some of master's degree. |
| Maya is 28 years old, Latina. She has four children. She completed high school. |
| Melanie is 29 years old, white. She has one child. She completed college. |
| Molly is 26 years old, white. She has one child. She has completed part of a Master's degree. |
| Morgan is 33 years old, white. She has two children. She completed part of a PhD. |
| Natalia is 28 years old, white. She has one child. She completed some college. |
| Nevaeh is 35 years old, black. She has three children. She completed the 9th grade. |
| Olivia is 18 years old, white. She has one child. She completed some college. |
| Rachel is 21 years old, white. She has one child. She completed the 11th grade. |
| Sabrina is 20 years old, Latina. RI. She has one child. She completed the 10th grade. |
| Sarah is 34 years old, white. She has three children. She completed high school. |
| Savannah is 29 years old, white. She has one child. She is currently in graduate school. |
| Sophia is 21 years old, Latina. She has two children. She completed high school. |
| Stella is 29 years old, Asian. She has one child. She has completed college. |
| Zoey is 28 years old, Latina. She has one child. She completed high school. |

*I assigned each participant a pseudonym based on the top 100 names in Rhode Island in 2010, which was the most recent available data from Social Security Online (www.socialsecurity.gov). This website provides the top 100 names by State and year of birth. The source is a 100% sample based on Social Security card application data.*

**Table 3.1 (cont.)**

avoiding pregnancy, the door to pregnancy might one day be opened, with a new set of unimagined challenges. As women wait longer to start "trying" to have a family, new doors to assisted reproductive technology are opened. Finally, first-time pregnant women may envision a closed door when they try to imagine what labor and delivery might be like for them. These closed doors represent a gap in the synergy of the self and the female body, which must be opened in order to eradicate the deficiencies in dialogue, knowledge, behaviors, and processes of the female body.

## *Chapter Four*

# Letting Go of Superwoman

## *Embodying the Mother-Child Dyad*

Aristotle described women as an empty vessel. Scholars trace the widespread belief that women's primary role is to serve as mothers to the writings of Aristotle (Blundell 2001). This philosophy emerged in Aeschylus' ancient Greek tragedy, *Eumenides*:

> The woman you call the mother of the child
> is not the parent, just a nurse to the seed,
> the new-sown seed that grows and swells inside her.
> The man is the source of life—the one who mounts.
> She, like a stranger for a stranger, keeps
> the shoot alive unless god hurts the roots. (658–61)

The notion of women as an empty vessel reduces women to their biological, reproductive role. In this view, women are essentialized and valued only in their ability to reproduce. As an empty vessel, women exist only to be filled. This metaphor persisted and is reflected in modern society in the popular television show *Friends*. In the episode "The One With All the Jealousy," Monica's boyfriend writes a poem entitled, "The Empty Vase." In the poem, he describes all women as empty vases: "My vessel so empty with nothing inside. Now that I've touched you, you seem emptier still" (Benson 1997). Even in contemporary U.S. popular culture, complicated understandings of women's functional role in society emerge, which essentialize women's bodies. As a vessel for future generations, women's bodies have been the source of centuries of medical attention.

This chapter builds on chapter 3 to understand how the mother-child dyad impacts women's meaning making of health. I present additional results from the same 44 conversations with women interviewed during the post-partum period. This chapter addresses (1) the physiological basis of reproductive health and motherhood, (2) perceptions of medicine and the biomedical model as a post-partum woman and mother, and (3) perceptions of media related to women's health and the health of children and families. This final chapter revisits themes of choice from chapter 1 as post-partum women make decisions about birth spacing and contraceptive methods. Quotes are a true representation of the participants' speech, with punctuation added to ease readability. Very few changes were made to ensure adequate communication of the participant's true meaning. Participants are identified with a pseudonym linked to their biographical profile in table 3.1.

Mothers of newborns provide a unique view of the duality of women's reproductive health. Particularly in the time period following the birth of a child, the health of mother and baby remain inextricably linked. The strong needs of the woman and the baby during this period highlights the dichotomy between the self and other. According to O'Grady (2004), "gender subordination is further reflected in the imbalance in many women's training between care for others and care for the self. Women traditionally have been assigned a disproportionate responsibility for the care of others" (95). The post-partum period requires the mother to take care of her own health in order to successfully care for her infant. The importance of personal health and self-care are challenged by the immediate and pressing needs of the baby. In this way, women may overlook their own health needs. Despite the importance of the mother's well-being in the post-partum period, the health care system often relegates women to the role of caretaker.

## THE PHYSIOLOGICAL BASIS OF REPRODUCTIVE HEALTH AND MOTHERHOOD

> "I try to take it easy instead of trying to be Superwoman." (Ava)

In the stories that follow, women questioned and reformulated traditional expectations of "putting the baby first." These women recognized that in order to care for their newborn, they first needed to care for themselves. Participants acknowledged the intrinsic duality of the mother-child dyad. According to a 33-year-old mother of two, "it is all connected. If I am healthy, I will have a healthy baby" (Morgan). Amelia, a 27-year-old new mother, agreed, "now, that I have a baby, the baby is a top priority. But, I also need to make myself a higher priority." These women discussed the importance of self-care in order to appropriately care for the health of the baby, "now, I have to take care of myself, so that I can take care of the baby. We both have to be healthy" (Zoey). Adriana, a 22-year-old first-time mother, described her thought process and the struggle to put her own health first, "I'm just thinking about taking care of her [newborn], I guess. I was thinking, her health is more important than mine. But, without mine, she can't be healthy. So, I guess she is my only way to stay healthy."

The role of mother influenced participants' imperative to stay healthy. Aubrey is a 25-year-old mother of two children. She had her first child at the age of 17 and was able to complete high school. She described the importance of health to fulfill her role as mother, "I'm more concerned about my kids. I don't do anything to put my health in jeopardy because it's all about my kids" (Aubrey). Another woman agreed, "now that I am a mom, I want to be hyper-vigilant about my health. I want to make sure I get enough sleep. I want to be healthy for the baby. I want to be there for the baby" (Isabella). These women also discussed the importance of improving their health or staying healthy in order to watch their children grow into adults.

Participants recognized and challenged the traditional expectation of "putting others first." These women struggled to overcome the expectation to be "Superwoman." One woman described this challenge, "for new moms, I think the newborn's health is often seen as more important than their own, which isn't good. . . . I totally get it, new moms feel overwhelmed and tired—your own health things take a back seat" (Allison). Participants described the importance of "me" time in order to avoid becoming overwhelmed and tired. For these biological mothers of newborns, "me" time meant "taking care of myself," "just getting away from my, well, kids sometimes," and "making sure I have time for my friends." These women also described the importance of not becoming overwhelmed by the new baby by protecting time to eat right, get enough sleep, and visit the doctor for preventive care.

Through conversations, participants made meaning of their health by reformulating the mother-child dyad, a process in which these women acknowledged the importance of their own health in caring for their child. In this way, women were able to "let go of being Superwoman" by recognizing the importance of "me" time in sustaining their physical and emotional health. These biological mothers of newborns embraced the duality of the mother-child dyad, which is essential for women's health because the health of mother and child are intrinsically linked (Brehaut et al. 2009).

## REVIVING THE SELF: PHYSICAL AND PSYCHOLOGICAL HEALTH

A variety of physical and psychological health issues emerged in discussions with biological mothers of newborns, including diet/exercise, reproductive health, chronic conditions, preventive care, and mental/emotional health. In

44 interviews, 159 unique health issues or topics were discussed by participants. Participants faced a variety of chronic conditions, which contributed to their understandings and opinions about health. These chronic conditions included orthopedic issues, anemia, dermatological concerns, migraines, scoliosis, irritable bowel syndrome (IBS), lupus, seizures, and multiple sclerosis. In some cases, these health concerns impacted the participant's view of her own health and how well she could care for her newborn. According to one woman, "imagine being a mother and being worried about having a seizure with him or him having a seizure eventually. But I don't really worry about it. I try not to. Well I don't have them very often" (Amaya). Another participant said, "unfortunately, my highest priority health issue is multiple sclerosis. If I don't take care of myself, everything else goes by the wayside. I have to be healthy for me and the kids" (Kaylee).

These women described the importance of preventive care, including regular doctor and dental visits, quitting smoking, learning about family history of disease in order to take measures to screen, prevent, and treat these diseases (e.g., Alzheimer's, Parkinson's, breast cancer, cervical cancer, diabetes, colon cancer, high blood pressure, kidney disease, asthma, leukemia, etc.), and preventing infectious disease (e.g., cold, flu, pertussis, etc.), such as through vaccinations and regular hand washing. Preventive care emerged as an important aspect of caring for self in order to care for children. Nevaeh is a 35-year-old black woman with a ninth-grade education and three children under the age of two. She described her fears related to preventive care, "when I think about health, I think I need to stop smoking. I would love to see my kids grow. If I keep smoking, I know there is a risk of not seeing them grow up" (Nevaeh).

Participants struggled with anxiety, obsessive compulsive disorder (OCD), and depression. Stigma and misunderstanding surrounding post-partum depression and the "baby blues" played an important role in understanding what it meant to be the mother of a newborn. Savannah is a 29-year-old first-time mother currently enrolled in graduate school. She described a lack of awareness of important mental health issues for new mothers:

> Especially in terms of "baby blues" or depression, I think it is important that people be able to distinguish the difference. Significant others should know what it's all about, I think sometimes it's minimized, especially people are so vulnerable after they have a baby.

Another woman discussed the importance of recognizing maternal health issues, especially post-partum depression, in order to provide appropriate care for a newborn:

> Getting your baby the care they need. If you have trouble, if you're struggling with depression, get help for yourself. Especially in light of that Coventry

> mother that smothered her baby. . . . You can sense the isolation and frustration. We've all been there, where we are so mad. Teaching moms to walk away. It's okay to leave your baby in the crib while you walk away for a minute, step outside, take deep breaths. Walk away and calm down, it's so important. Only takes a minute. (Khloe)

## THE CONSTANT CONVERSATION: DIET AND THE BODY

Each participant was asked to identify her highest priority health issue. Most participants identified diet or nutrition and exercise as an important health issue and this topic emerged as the highest priority health issue for many participants. Twenty-five of 44 participants identified diet and nutrition or exercise as their highest priority health issue. Participants mentioned diet and nutrition or exercise 101 times throughout the interviews. Specifically, these women defined their highest priority health issue as the constant conversation of diet and the body, including losing weight and body image, interpretation of medical authority and listening to the body, and integration of maternal and child health. Many women associated health with food and diet. They described varied cultural understandings and practices related to food. "Eating right" was identified as the "most important thing" and these women described themselves as "focused on" or "obsessed with" diet and exercise. According to Sarah, a 34-year-old mother of three, "I am really worried about my diet right now" (Sarah). Participants discussed issues of diet and exercise as their primary health concern. Losing weight was closely tied to understandings of the body, body image, and being a woman or mother. Women also described the challenge of waiting to exercise following delivery until an arbitrary deadline imposed on her body by doctors.

For some women, health was synonymous with diet and nutrition. According to one woman, "when I think of health, I think of food" (Maya). Another participant reinforced the link between healthy eating and the body, "when I think about health, I think about the body—being healthy, living a healthy lifestyle. . . . Eating right is my biggest thing" (Alexa). Many women described a history of being "concerned about" diet and nutrition. According to Gia, a 35-year-old first time mom, "I've always been concerned about my weight. . . . As long as I can get out and hike or kayak and do what I want. Those are my driving factors for health."

Many women were guided by traditional, cultural understandings of food and diet. According to one participant, "I stay healthy by eating good food. I eat Mediterranean food, so I don't have to think about my diet" (Morgan). Another woman said:

> For me, I think the most important health topic is food. I eat a lot of vegetables, meat, and fish. When I go home, I forget about what I eat. It just becomes natural, normal. Asians follow what the body needs—we eat a lot of rice. But, I've gotten used to the food here. I try a lot of the different food here. And I don't have allergies really, but there are differences between food here and at home. (Stella)

Participants described the importance of losing weight in relation to body image and being a woman or mother. Many women acknowledged the problematic societal emphasis on losing weight among women and particularly the mothers of newborns. Addison, a 40-year-old mother of three children, described the prevalence of discussions among women about diet, where the focus is on "just losing weight now. I definitely want to get back to where I was. . . . I don't want to stay this way. . . . It's like a constant conversation with women, I swear. How do we lose weight?" Another participant reinforced the ubiquity of weight in the lives of women, while acknowledging that too much emphasis may be problematic, "I guess for me, women always think of their weight when they think of being healthy. I definitely paid attention to my weight, not too much attention, but I think that's a good gauge of how you're doing health-wise" (Madeline).

Many women challenged the societal norm emphasizing losing weight among women and new mothers. According to one participant, "right now, I am mostly thinking about exercise, losing weight is always kind of, all women are never really satisfied. I think many mothers are focused on losing weight, unfortunately. I'm like, 'dude, you just had a baby, relax'" (Savannah). Participants suggested that this focus on weight loss and body image may be detrimental to overall women's health. According to Amaya, a 29-year-old Latina mother of two children, "the important thing is to do it [lose weight] right. Some people just get silly and ignore themselves health-wise to get back down. Vanity. That's the only general thing about it. People worrying what they look like. Thinking about their man" (Amaya).

Other participants described the importance of losing weight in order to fulfill their role as a mother. According to one woman, "weight loss—I think about that stuff all the time. I'm a mom. When I think of my health, I just think about not being overweight. At a comfortable weight I should say" (Ava). Emma, a 26-year-old mother of three children, described the importance of losing weight to be able to play with her children, "as soon as I am all healed up, I want to be healthier, so we can all play together."

Women also associated weight loss with medical advice in order to avoid pregnancy-related complications. According to one participant,

> in terms of my health, I have hypertension. My mom has diabetes. I knew that I needed to lose weight. But then, the baby came along. While I was pregnant, I found out that I had gestational diabetes. I am planning to get pregnant again,

> so, I need to lose enough weight, so that I don't get gestational diabetes next time. (Caroline)

The body emerged as a site where women's identity formed in relation to gender and reproduction. According to O'Grady (2004),

> two factors typical of many women's experience—the cultural legacy of subordinate status and an imbalance between care for others and care for the self—that are likely to enhance the power of self-policing. Such forces encourage women to live according to the expectations of others, which both reflects and heightens vulnerability to practices of self-surveillance and self-evaluation. (91)

Kline (2011) found that media representations perpetuated gender stereotypes related to health issues, including the expectation that women maintain expertise in dieting and nutrition. As a result, women self-police and self-punish through "the imposition of punishing forms of exercise or food deprivation if body weight is perceived to exceed mainstream culture's relentless expectation for slim girls and women" (O'Grady 2004, 96–97).

In this study, women acknowledged the problematic emphasis on weight loss and body image placed on them by society. At the same time, most of these participants continued to see diet/nutrition and/or exercise as their highest priority health issue, even when health was not their primary motivating factor for losing weight. In this way, participants may have experienced a false consciousness, which occurs when individuals' common sense understandings reinforce oppressive dominant ideologies (Lather 1991). Gramsci's theories of hegemony, which he developed in the 1920s and 1930s, suggest that individuals hold beliefs that do not serve their best interest (Gramsci 1971). False consciousness reinforces the importance of hegemony in understanding diet/nutrition and/or exercise as participants' highest priority health issue.

## REPRODUCTION: BEYOND THE WANDERING WOMB

The body's centrality to the physical process and cultural understanding of reproduction requires investigation of the body as a central feature of analysis. Ettorre (2000) uses the body as the point of analysis and theorizes on reproductive genetics, arguing that reproductive genetics obscures the role of the environment and gendered social practices in the identification of "defective genes," which exist in a context of the medicalization of health and illness. This interpretation of the pathologized female body in pregnancy as a reflection of the gendered social practices and the pursuit of a genetic normal underlines the relationship of social norms surrounding gender and the body with the physical and biological constructs of the body.

The father of modern medicine, Hippocrates, and the ancient philosophers Aristotle and Plato played a distinctive role in current societal norms and values surrounding gender and the body. Aristotle believed in the essential inferiority of the female: "'a woman is, as it were, an infertile man. She is female in fact on account of a kind of inadequacy' (Generation of animals 728a)" (Blundell 2001, 106). Woman's inadequacy stemmed from her ability to reproduce, and one specific body part: her uterus or womb.

According to Blundell (2001), the "ideological interpretation of a women's illness in ancient Greece: the restlessness of the womb is suggestive of a basic physiological instability to which a woman inevitably falls victim unless a man intervenes in her life" (101). This instability causes a variety of ailments, which may only be cured through pregnancy. In this way, reproduction serves as both the disease and the cure. The restlessness of the womb causes illness by wandering around the body:

> A graphic account of its cause is supplied by one of the characters in a dialogue by Plato, who tells us that the womb is an animal within a woman, which is desirous of bearing children (Timaeus 91). If this desire remains unsatisfied for a long time, the womb becomes restless and starts to wander about the body; as a consequence, the passages for breath become blocked, and this causes distress and "disorders of all kinds." The problem will continue until the woman has sex with a man and becomes pregnant. (Blundell 2001, 100)

The restlessness of the womb confines women to their reproductive role.

The wandering womb can be traced through contemporary ideology in the political and social institutions that essentialize women and reduce them to their biological function. In 1963, Friedan identified "the problem that has no name" as the feminine mystique, which suggested that women should be happy fulfilling their biological roles as housewives and mothers (Friedan 2001). Friedan's critique of functionalism ushered in second-wave feminism in the United States. The legacy of the wandering womb and functionalism on women's lives served to silence women's voices.

As mothers of newborns, reproductive health and fertility emerged as health issues at the forefront of many participants' minds. They described their struggles with infertility, including miscarriage and polycystic ovarian disease. Reflecting Bute's (2009) research on conversations about infertility, participants described being silenced by taboos around women's health topics, such as miscarriage. According to Natalia, a 28-year-old first-time mother, "I was very concerned about my reproductive health. I had a couple ovarian surgeries. I was very concerned I wouldn't be able to have children." Other women described challenges they faced during pregnancy, such as gestational diabetes and preeclampsia. Participants also described the importance of post-partum healing and adjusting to the new baby.

Looking to the future, these women described the role of contraception and birth spacing in their lives. Participants used a variety of contraceptive methods prior to pregnancy, including the birth control pill, injection, intrauterine device (IUD), and withdrawal. According to Sophia, a 21-year-old mother of two children,

> twelve months ago, I probably had birth control methods in mind that I possibly could have taken. At the time, I was trying to get pregnant. I really wasn't too knowledged on birth control methods. I was taking a birth control pill. I purposely stopped taking it, to get pregnant.

These women often invited me to stay and listen during their midwife consultation. The midwife was an employee of the hospital and employed a standard checklist of questions to prepare mothers of newborns to go home. The midwife asked a number of questions, including, "what is your plan for contraception?" One mother responded, "my husband and I usually just wing it." The midwife replied, "well, you have options: condoms would be an option or withdrawal." The mother responded, "Yes, we use withdrawal." The midwife said, "well, withdrawal is about 80% effective." The midwife offered to administer a birth control injection before the new mother left the hospital. The new mother declined. A number of these women described the offer of a birth control injection prior to discharge. Many participants refused the birth control injection. According to Aubrey, "they asked me if I wanted to get a shot before I leave. I don't want to get pregnant right away but I have to wait 6 weeks to get Mirena [IUD]. So, I have to avoid sex." The IUD may be inserted immediately following vaginal birth or caesarean section; however, women receive conflicting information about this option (Sundstrom, Szabo, and Dempsey 2014). A number of participants described their intention to undergo female sterilization. According to Nevaeh, "I have three children under two. I plan to get my tubes tied. I'm tired of being pregnant. I just want to be me again. I want to have the strength to take care of my children."

## RESISTING THE BIOMEDICAL MODEL

Women resisted the biomedical model in a variety of ways. Some of this resistance emerged subtly, by expressing preference for one health care provider over another. According to one participant, "my OB is really good. My PCP, the last time I talked to him was freshman year in college. So, technically my OB is my PCP. Little things here and there, I will ask my OB" (Caroline). Addison described a great relationship with her physician that was overshadowed by the nurse practitioner, "I think [my physician] really knows what he's talking about. He's so great. But actually, it's like, this nurse practitioner, she's just amazing so, you just want to go in there for anything." Another participant preferred her midwife:

> I really like my midwife. I prefer her over my doctor. [Why?] She just listens more. The doctor I have doesn't listen. She comes in and chit chats about anything and the doctor doesn't listen to anything I say. She takes the time to actually hear what I have to say so it's much better. It works. (Camila)

Some women resisted the biomedical paradigm by avoiding their doctor, when possible. According to Alexa, "my general provider plays zero role in my personal health. I see her once a year. A once a year check-up and that is it." Another participant described her highest priority health issue, mental and emotional health, "my doctor is, not a last resort, but I have a lot of other coping strategies that I use before I feel like I need to talk to a doctor" (Madeline).

Some women viewed the doctor-patient relationship as a "hassle" and described a complex process for interpreting advice from a physician, while taking responsibility for their own health decisions. According to one participant, "sometimes you don't want to go through the hassle of calling the doctor, getting in the car, and going over there" (Alyssa). Another woman described her relationship with her physicians as, "good on a basic level. Nothing personal. [What role do they play in your health?] An advisor, I guess. Your general health is your responsibility. But they can advise you on topics, questions, anything you have" (Amaya). Hannah is a 22-year-old mother of four children with a tenth-grade education. She described how she managed chronic back pain without advice from a doctor, "I haven't talked to nobody about it. I just try to take care of it by myself at home. I just get some heating pads. I'll take some pain medications to see if it'll go away."

Some participants resisted the medical model by questioning diagnoses and medical recommendations. Other women supplemented physicians' opinions with outside information or disagreed with medical advice. One participant described how she resisted her physician's explanation of irritable bowel syndrome (IBS):

> I have a gastroenterologist, but he doesn't really explain what is going on in a good way. I went in to see him and he says I have some sort of metabolic something syndrome. He says, "you have this, this, this, this." And I am like, "But what does that mean?" So, I have to look it up. (Caroline)

Amelia discussed how she questioned her doctor's suggestions. She said, "for everything the doctor recommended I take, any medications or vitamins during pregnancy, I always asked about the importance of taking it and what's in it and what it's for. I wanted to know the importance of taking it."

Participants described the experience of disagreeing with their physician and the importance of the interpersonal relationship. According to Amaya,

> general bedside manner is very important. Even if you come to disagreements, the bedside manner makes all the difference. I had one doctor tell me that if I didn't start taking my meds, I was going to die. That is exactly how she said it, "You're going to die if you don't take this." So that's bedside manner.

Another participant said, "I've disagreed with my primary care physician, definitely. Like anyone you would ask for advice, you take the advice you were given and evaluate how much you are likely to agree with it or disagree" (Madeline).

## LISTENING TO THE BODY

The role of medical authority also emerged in participants' understandings of how much they could exercise and what they could eat during pregnancy, and when they could exercise after delivery. Participants described conflicting understandings and approaches to exercise during pregnancy. One participant suggested that exercising could be harmful to a developing fetus, "twelve months ago, I was trying to get pregnant. So, I was exercising less because I didn't want to jostle the baby" (Morgan).

The biomedical paradigm and medical authority conflicted with women's instincts to listen to their body. This finding builds on research conducted by Warren and Brewis (2004), which described pregnancy as a body episode, in which women are able to live outside cultural expectations for the female body. Participants in this study suggested that while pregnancy may offer a reprieve from cultural stereotypes of womanhood and beauty, these expectations may be replaced by equally oppressive and unjustified medical dictums.

Medicalization of women's bodies emerged as participants described a contest over their bodies in relation to diet and exercise before, during, and after pregnancy. This finding reinforced Kline's (2006) argument that women's bodies have been medicalized so that natural processes, such as pregnancy, are understood as illnesses. These women rebelled against the assumption of pathology intrinsic to their bodies, which relegated these natural processes to medical authority (Foucault 1978). Participants described the role of body image and weight loss in relation to "getting my body back" and "becoming myself again." In this way, participants lived the duality of women's reproductive health and challenged the connection between self and body. Women in this study described their struggle to reclaim their bodies and empower themselves culturally through the singular action of personifying themselves and their bodies as one (e.g., Sartre; Merleau-Ponty).

Participants described a variety of approaches to fitness and exercise during pregnancy. One woman aptly summarized the challenge that pregnant women face in regard to understanding and choosing healthy exercise options:

> I would like to know more about exercising, and what, certain exercises you can do while you are pregnant, during and after pregnancy. And eating on a daily basis—what maybe some foods you should stay away from, like if you are eating fish, only eat a certain amount, or only eat this kind of fish. Just how to keep a good, balanced diet. (Sophia)

Some participants described the importance of staying active throughout pregnancy. According to Faith, a 40-year-old mother of four children, "I like walking a lot. I actually went hiking all throughout my pregnancy up until six or seven months. I look forward to exercising again. I haven't talked to my doctor about it yet." Other women described their inability to continue with an exercise program as a result of pregnancy. One woman said, "I miss my women's cardio kickboxing class. It was high intensity, so I couldn't do it during pregnancy. I can't wait to get back to that" (Molly).

Participants described the role that physicians play in dictating the acceptability of exercise during and after pregnancy. One woman described how a medical restriction during pregnancy drastically changed her physical activity regimen:

> Nutrition and exercise are really important to me. I exercise as much as possible. I used to go to the YMCA. I would do Pilates and yoga. Before I got pregnant, I was training to run a 10K, that was my top of mind exercise goal. I had a running schedule and I was mixing in other exercises to build up endurance. Then, when I got pregnant, I had placenta previa and they [my doctor] restricted my exercise. I was only allowed to walk, walk around the block, I couldn't do the treadmill, couldn't do Pilates. It was hard, that was my kind of outlet, that was "me" time. I'm not a big hobby person. I tried reading. I started scrapbooking for my daughter. Just trying to fill the void that exercise filled. (Ariana)

Some women challenged the arbitrary six- or eight-week resting period post-delivery. According to one participant, "running, which I miss so much, I hope to get back into it soon. . . . They said six weeks. But, I am just going to try to listen to my body. I'm just going to see how my body feels" (Kaylee). Another woman felt ready to run after only a couple of weeks, however, she reinforced the importance of the doctor's "okay" to resume her preferred exercise, "now I cannot wait. It is eight weeks for the c-section. I really feel like running now. When I have my six-week with the doctor, I'm going to ask him if I can start a little early" (Isabella).

Women focused on diet and nutrition while they waited to resume exercising. According to Allison, "well, I need to reinvigorate my nutrition and exercise after the pregnancy. I had a c-section, so I have to wait to exercise. But, I am focusing on a balanced diet." Another participant said, "next month, I will be able to exercise again. It is okay because I know my body needs to wait. I didn't think nothing of it, I just knew my body needed to wait" (Aaliyah).

Women resisted the biomedical paradigm in various ways, such as through trusting their bodies and valuing storytelling and personal narrative as a form of expertise. Participants described interpersonal communication with their physician as a central communication channel related to their highest priority health issue. However, participants resisted the medical model in a variety of ways. Some participants resisted the medical model by questioning diagnoses and medical recommendations, supplementing physicians' opinions with outside information, or disagreeing with medical advice. This finding contributes to research on medicalization (Kline 2006; Martin 2001; Pollock 1999) by further explicating how women make meaning of the biomedical paradigm and the ways that they question and resist medical authority.

## PERCEPTIONS OF MEDIA

Biological mothers of newborns identified mediated health messages related to: (1) diet, nutrition, and/or exercise and (2) topics integrating maternal and child health. These women evaluated the health behavior and audience targeted by the campaign, along with the message's strategy and content. In addition to their highest priority health issues, participants also discussed campaigns around anti-smoking, a secondary health issue for some participants, and charity events. Although anti-smoking emerged as a ubiquitous campaign, some women disliked the strategy and content of the ads. According to one participant, "I think that anti-tobacco ads are inappropriate, most of them, they are off-putting, they try to go way too far making their point" (Ariana).

These women described seeing advertisements and recruitment for charity events, mainly in the form of health walks. They believed that these events raised their awareness around certain health issues, however, all of the women who took part in these events described their participation related to a family member who suffered from the illness. According to one woman, "on Facebook. . . . I don't really connect with companies or hospitals. But I did join the Relay for Life group because I personally have family members impacted by [cancer]" (Allison). Another participant said, "I walked for diabetes and have done different walks like that. Oh, I walked for Alzheimer's. My grandfather has Alzheimer's" (Mackenzie).

These women identified mediated messages related to diet and exercise surrounding *Let's Move!* Michelle Obama's campaign targeting childhood obesity in an effort to raise a healthier generation of kids. The goals of the campaign are to encourage children and families to eat healthy and get active. The campaign focuses on food and nutrition, as well as physical activity. Participants believed the campaign's target audience, children, was important to the success of the campaign. Morgan, a 33-year-old mother of two children, described the world her newborn daughter will grow up in:

> Her generation is so different from ours. Her foods will already have hormones. We will be healthier than them. Just like, I guess, our parents were healthier than us. But, it just makes it more important to focus on exercise and eating good. It's important for her to have less sugar, less fat. It is the best way to avoid being sick. And diseases, like diabetes, high cholesterol and things like that.

Overall, participants supported the campaign's health behavior. According to one woman,

> Michelle Obama is doing the vegetable gardens to get healthier food into schools. So that is the campaign that stands out. Obviously, everyone looks up to Michelle Obama and respects her. The fact that she's in the school lunches for me is wonderful because that's my daughter's imminent future. When I was in high school, the soda machine was open all the time. Now, you'd be hard-pressed to find a soda machine in any school and that's great. (Khloe)

Participants supported the strategy and content of the campaign. In particular, women associated the campaign with Michelle Obama and believed that her celebrity status was an effective strategy to gain attention and awareness. One participant described the campaign as "the whole Michelle Obama thing" (Isabella) and another said, "public figures, celebrities, the first lady, brings it more in the public eye" (Allison). One woman described disagreeing with the campaign's behavior change strategies, noting, "unfortunately, I don't think they are too effective. I think statistics are effective because they scare people" (Alexa).

Participants identified Got Milk? as a health campaign targeting diet and nutrition. Got Milk? is funded by the MilkPEP (Milk Processor Education Program), which is made up of the nation's milk processors, who are committed to increasing fluid milk consumption. Although this may not fulfill the definition of a traditional social marketing campaign, it is important to understand participants' views about this advertising campaign. Kaylee, a 36-year-old mother of two children, said, "the only campaign I can think of is the Got Milk? campaign. Obviously it stuck with me. It was good, the overall appeal, health for everyone." Although many women favored the Got Milk? campaign, some were also skeptical of the campaign's motives. According to one participant,

> I always take it with a grain of salt because I feel like anything that is pushing a particular trend or particular topic is probably biased in some way or another and if you're going to buy into it, you really need to spend time evaluating the whole idea and finding out how much truth there is to that particular campaign because more than likely it's not as straightforward as it seems. (Madeline)

Participants described the integration of maternal and child health, particularly in the area of feeding, as one of their highest priority health issues for their newborn. In this area, participants described seeing health messages targeting breastfeeding, pregnancy, and developing an attachment to the newborn through the First Hug campaign. According to one participant, "campaigns are effective when they use people who they are regarding, having an interest, related to them" (Savannah). This explanation describes participants' attention and interest in the March of Dimes campaigns surrounding pregnancy, prematurity, and birth defects. According to one woman, "I saw a lot [of campaigns] by the March of Dimes. Other than that. . . . I'm sure there were some wonderful ones I probably read, but I was consumed with the pregnancy, so I only read things pertaining to that" (Natalia). Participants described extensive promotion of breastfeeding. One woman said, "I remember seeing all breastfeeding campaigns. They said it is healthy for the baby and for me too. They are very informative and there is a lot of promoting of it, just tells you more about it" (Faith).

The five approaches to feeding infants described by women in this study include breastfeeding, breastfeeding and pumping, pumping only, supplementing breast milk with formula, and formula only. Many participants felt intense pressure to breastfeed. These women described social stigma and guilt if they were unable or decided not to breastfeed (Sundstrom 2014). There were many reasons participants chose not to breastfeed, including contraindicated medications, health issues of the baby or the mother, limited time off from school or work, as well as desiring the assistance of their partner in feeding.

The divisive issue of breastfeeding continues to receive scholarly and popular attention. Breastfeeding has been explored as a feminist and public health issue. According to Blum (2000), "postmodern and poststructural scholars instruct us that bodily practices—despite their undeniable physicality—are always historical. In other words, our meaning-making practices shape how we see, interpret, and treat the body" (2). Breastfeeding is situated in a history of inadvertent stigma in health communication campaigns aimed at controlling women's bodies (Gurrieri, Previte, and Brace-Govan 2013). According to Barston (2012), bottle feeding has become "the mark of bad motherhood" to the extent that "we have muffled the voices of women who may not want to nurse and have insisted that their feelings are invalid, merely the result of formula marketing rather than legitimate concerns about body and autonomy" (11). The government, "lactivists," and special interest groups, such as the La Leche League, promote the social imperative to breastfeed.

Morris (2014) reveals "how the scientific case for the benefits of breast-feeding has been oversold by the people we trust to advise us, and why formula will not make your child fat, sick or stupid" (5). According to Wolf (2010),

> while compelling evidence indicates that breastfeeding reduces babies' risk for various gastrointestinal (GI) infections, medical journals are otherwise replete with contradictory conclusions about breastfeeding's impact: for every piece of research linking it to better health, another finds it to be irrelevant, weakly significant, or inextricably tied to factors that are difficult to measure. (xii)

For example, through an analysis of over 80 breastfeeding studies over the last two decades, researchers at the Cincinnati Children's Medical Center failed to find conclusive evidence that breastfeeding reduces obesity prevalence in children (Woo and Martin 2015). Another recent study investigated a nationally representative sample of siblings who were fed differently as infants and identified no statistically significant benefit of breastfeeding on indicators of health and well-being up to age 14 (Colen and Ramey 2014). These findings reinforce the importance of understanding the unintended consequences of health communication campaign messages.

The most salient health messages for participants included the First Hug or Skin-to-Skin campaign. This campaign focuses on developing an attachment to the newborn. Nevaeh said, "skin-to-skin, I had my baby like that. The nurse said it was so the baby can hear you and be loved by you. That one makes you think." Another woman described how she found out about it from the nurse in the delivery room: "it was really comforting, it is good they have that information available to you. It was a very wonderful experience, and for me to be able to regulate his body temperature on me" (Sophia). Many women noted that they had not had the opportunity to have a first hug with previous children. Aubrey said, "we had our first hug for two hours. It worked. There was a connection. He could smell me and know I was his mom. It felt good. I didn't know about it with my first daughter. It was useful."

These women heard about the first hug from a variety of sources, including WIC counselors, nurses, family, and friends. One woman said, "skin-to-skin is everywhere. I did it. It was good. It was a lot more bonding, it seemed to work much better compared to my other births" (Faith). Another participant said, "I did skin-to-skin this morning. I like this. It makes my baby more comfortable. My family, my sister told me about it too, before I got to the hospital" (Zoey). Women who were unable to breastfeed appreciated the opportunity to bond with their newborn. According to one woman, "for me, its very interesting that I can still do the same thing and get that bonding. That's something I liked and I started doing it as soon as the nurse said I could" (Amaya).

Women described the role of medical authority in determining whether or not mothers would be able to have a first hug with their newborn. Some participants heard about this campaign from their nurse. One woman said, "nurses are the front line defense to get information out there" (Ariana). Another participant expressed concern about the role of nurses in this campaign:

> I heard about skin-to-skin in the recovery room. My WIC counselor actually told me about it too. She said the first hour is the most important. I didn't realize that. But I have a friend who came to have a baby. And the lady, the nurse just lifted her gown and plopped the baby down. So, I think its good, but it has to be your choice. (Emma)

Some women were prohibited from having immediate skin-to-skin contact with their newborn. According to Isabella, a 39-year-old first-time mother, "I was a little upset that I couldn't do the first hug. I understand that it is what they needed to do—bring him over to the NICU. I would have liked to have that initial skin-to-skin contact."

Participants evaluated the health behavior and audience targeted by health messages, along with the strategy and content. Participants suggested that mediated health messages were most successful when they closely aligned with their interests. These women sought opportunities to "personalize" campaigns by signing up for specific information or events. Participants also described the importance of well-known organizational or celebrity "names" supporting or endorsing the campaign. Participants were more likely to understand and identify with messages that offered multiple perspectives on an issue. These findings suggest the importance of understanding the target audience and, to the extent possible, providing tailored, personalized campaign messages.

# Conclusion

Reproductive rights are human rights. According to Betty Friedan (2001), "the *personhood* of women, that's what it's really all about, first and finally" (73). A national and global discourse about the personhood of women underscores the belief that women's right to life, health, and privacy depends on the ability to determine if, when, and how to have children. According to Haraway (2004), "cyborg writing is about the power to survive, not on the basis of original innocence, but on the basis of seizing the tools to mark the world that marked them as other" (33). Through stories and silence, the women interviewed in this book shared a crucial component of ensuring reproductive rights: accurate information about reproductive health and access to services and technology.

This book contributes to a culture-centered approach to public health research and practice, which is paramount in developing effective health communication campaigns. In line with van Zoonen (1994) "the final aim remains to reconstruct people's experiences and interpretations on their own terms" (136). By talking with women, this study privileges the voices of individual women and allows their stories and understandings to emerge. According to Sharf et al. (2011), "these narrative forms offer different ways of understanding the lived experiences of others while also challenging conventional representations and prevailing assumptions" (45).

This book contributes to recent efforts to develop a "life course" perspective to address women's health. *Women's Voices* investigates four critical body episodes: contraceptive use dynamics, pregnancy, childbirth, and the post-partum period. Women's meaning making of each body episode is interrogated in three areas: (1) the physiological experience of reproductive health, (2) perceptions of medicine and the biomedical model, and (3) perceptions of mediated messages about reproduction, including new media.

This analysis reaffirms that "there are grounds for hope in the emerging bases for new kinds of unity across race, gender, and class" (Haraway, 2004, 30), especially if women embrace the possibility of science and technology and are "not afraid of permanently partial identities and contradictory standpoints" (Haraway 2004, 13).

Women deserve better information about the risks and benefits of medicine and health care. The importance of accurate, unbiased scientific information is exemplified in women's decision making about screening. Intuitive thought and assumptions about the linearity of disease impact social norms and communication about the benefits of screening. However, the risk of false positives and overdiagnosis is a major harm associated with screening programs. As a result, the true costs of screening must include the adverse effects experienced by patients, such as anxiety, pain, psychological distress, and negative outcomes associated with diagnostic follow-up procedures. When physicians and risk communicators discuss early disease detection in terms of relative risk reduction, they tend to overstate the benefits of screening. Absolute risk rather than relative risk is the most accurate way to discuss screening and to support consumer-oriented informed medical decision making.

In chapter 1, communication and understanding of risk impacted how women made decisions about contraception. Although approximately 70% of pregnancies among young unmarried women ages 20 to 29 are unplanned, social norms and a lack of knowledge limit the contraceptive choices of these women. Narratives about the risk of contraception tend to disregard or downplay the risks of pregnancy and childbirth. Furthermore, these narratives omit the fact that hormonal contraception offers a net health benefit to users, in addition to pregnancy prevention (Hannaford et al. 2010; Vessey, Yeates, and Flynn 2010). Long-acting reversible contraceptive methods, including the intrauterine device (IUD) and implant, are 99% effective with typical use, offer the opportunity to improve women's health, and decrease unintended pregnancy. Health communication campaigns should highlight that the oral contraceptive pill is only 91% effective with typical use. Messages about LARC should emphasize the safety of continuous use of hormonal contraception and menstrual suppression including decreasing the risk of certain cancers and improving fertility. The noncontraceptive benefits of these options should also be addressed. According to Takeshita (2014), "As with other lifestyle drugs, modifying the material body with menstrual suppression products produces culturally and socially meaningful positive changes in the identities and lives of their users" (254). In other words, risks must be reconceptualized outside of the normative "natural" processes of menstruation, pregnancy, and childbirth.

An emerging issue in contraception is the bipartisan effort to move oral contraception over-the-counter (OTC). According to Grossman et al. (2013),

OTC access to OCPs is safe, effective, and supported by women who would obtain refills or start using OCPs if they were available over-the-counter. In the current study, participants described going to the doctor and dealing with insurance and the pharmacy as "really annoying." These young women frequently described going on vacation or moving away for the summer and being unable to pick up their prescription in a timely manner. These struggles suggest that college-age women would be interested in purchasing OCPs from their local pharmacy without a doctor's visit or prescription.

The second chapter explored the medicalization of pregnancy. In particular, women's stories explicated how the focus on preventing pregnancy for more than a decade of their reproductive life obscures and limits women's understanding of what it really means to live in the body. In this study, pregnant women desired shared decision making with health care providers to make complex choices from genetic testing to cord blood banking. According to Haraway (2004),

> ambivalence toward the disrupted unities mediated by high-tech culture requires not sorting consciousness into categories of "clear-sighted critique grounding a solid political epistemology" versus "manipulated false consciousness," but subtle understanding of emerging pleasures, experiences, and powers with serious potential for changing the rules of the game. (30)

In preparation for labor and delivery, many women sought a middle ground between a hospital and home birth, preferring alternative birthing centers.

Almost one-third of all women in the United States give birth by cesarean delivery, which imposes a significant burden on the health and well-being of women and infants, as well as the health care system. In chapter 3, medicalization of women's bodies emerged as participants described a contest over their bodies before, during, and after pregnancy. The biomedical paradigm and medical authority conflicted with women's instincts to listen to their body. Participants described how improving their satisfaction with childbirth will require strategies that empower women by providing accurate information, including the risks and benefits of interventions, and decision making tools to make informed choices.

Participants felt intense pressure to breastfeed. These women described social stigma and guilt if they were unable or decided not to breastfeed. Women resisted the biomedical paradigm in various ways, such as through trusting their bodies and valuing storytelling and personal narrative as a form of expertise. In chapter 4, participants described interpersonal communication with their physician as a central communication channel related to their highest priority health issue. However, participants resisted the medical model in a variety of ways. Some participants resisted the medical model by questioning diagnoses and medical recommendations, supplementing physicians' opinions with outside information, or disagreeing with medical advice.

## TECHNOLOGY TROUBLE

In October 2014, media outlets reported that major technology companies Apple and Facebook offered egg freezing in their health insurance benefits packages. Egg freezing or human oocyte cryopreservation allows a woman's eggs (oocytes) to be extracted, frozen, and stored. This procedure has been effective in helping cancer patients preserve their fertility before chemotherapy. In 2012, the American Society for Reproductive Medicine removed the experimental label from the procedure, however, it is still not recommended for healthy women who want to delay pregnancy.

Although there is no guarantee that frozen eggs will be successful in creating a future pregnancy, research suggests that young eggs reduce the risk of miscarriage and genetic defects, such as Down syndrome. In 2014, a number of news outlets, including the *New York Post* and the *Huffington Post* ran stories about women in their thirties attending "egg freezing parties" to learn more about the procedure.

Apple and Facebook's decision to include egg freezing in their health insurance plan led to a backlash among some feminists, who argued that the benefit was designed to coerce women to postpone pregnancy and focus on their careers. The debate inspired conversations about work-life balance, maternity benefits, childcare, and the need for a more comprehensive conversation about parenting in the United States. Surprisingly, there was little feminist discussion about the opportunity for egg freezing technology to empower women. In fact, the technology companies cover a full range of reproductive health services, including surrogacy. According to Weber (2014),

> in my view, it is quite important that feminist studies continue to elaborate that *the technical is the political* for all the divergent fields of science and technology, showing and analyzing the ongoing co-construction of gender, science, and technology. In order to take part in the shaping of contemporary sociotechnical practices and discourses, we need to engage with today's scientific, cultural, and social turbulences, to engage in contests about what counts as nature, intelligible bodies, or efficient machines. To question techno-pragmatic and hegemonic forms of rationality and the dominant logic of efficiency, usability, and common sense, we need to intervene and challenge hierarchical sociotechnical relations by developing new theories of our age of technoscience. (554)

It is interesting that feminist scholars and activists failed to recognize how these reproductive technologies might help women to escape from the reproductive economy.

According to the Center for Reproductive Rights, all women have the right to benefit from scientific progress. Reproductive technologies, such as contraception, egg freezing, *in vitro* fertilization, and surrogacy, have the opportunity to improve women's lives and reproductive health. According to Wyer et al. (2014),

> in the United States many issues that would be resolved if women were recognized as fully entitled to constitutional protections continue to plague us. Debates about public funding of birth control, women's health services, and constitutional rights to privacy and same-sex marriage, for instance, continue to reveal deep societal ambivalences about whether women really ought to be full citizens with all the rights, privileges, and responsibilities of men. (xx–xxi)

Scientific progress also includes access to knowledge about the risks of medicalized reproduction, including cesarean section. The stories in this book articulate how women make meaning of the complexities of their reproductive health. Their lived experiences advocate for the necessity of accurate information, including the risks and benefits of reproductive technologies, and access to all services and technologies.

Social expectations define and limit women's reproductive role, often dictating women's understanding of their bodies. The word "pregnant," from the Latin *gravidus*, meaning "loaded," emerged from *gravis*, or "burdened, heavy" (Merriam-Webster 2004, 547). The burden of pregnancy is reflected in the struggles of infertility. When the Hippocratic remedies for infertility failed, women in ancient Greece relied on other means to fulfill their reproductive role:

> If all else failed, then a desperate woman might have recourse to the black market in babies, at least if the comic playwright Aristophanes is to be believed. In a catalogue of crafty dodges perpetrated by women, one example cited is that of a woman who had to keep up a sham labour for ten days while the midwife was looking for a suitable child. Eventually a baby was brought home concealed in a jar; the husband was hurried out of the room, the beeswax which had been used to stop the baby's mouth was removed, the baby cried, and everyone was delighted (Thesmophoriazusae 502–18). (Blundell 2001, 106)

Today, women experiencing infertility seek assisted reproductive technology, surrogacy, and adoption. These techniques are mirrored in the Hippocratic infertility remedies and the black market, to which women in ancient Greece turned.

Approaches to infertility and reproduction reflect societal norms. According to Blizzard (2007), the meaning of technological innovations during pregnancy, such as in utero surgery, are culturally constructed by patients, their social networks, and health care providers. Bute and Jensen (2010) examined the norms of fertility and pregnancy among low-income women to compare and contrast “mainstream” societal norms. The findings suggest that while peer-oriented norms and subgroup expectations inform perceptions of fertility and the body, these norms generally correspond with mainstream descriptive norms. This finding is notable for demonstrating the commonalities of perceptions among subgroups while also describing the more insular process of the formation of those perceptions, which leaves the possibility that norms could diverge and health-related behaviors affected by targeting peer-to-peer education in subpopulations.

This study builds on theoretical work examining power, control, and hegemony as regulatory controls of the body and reproduction (Foucault 1978). According to Butler (2010),

> there is no ontology of gender on which we might construct a politics, for gender ontologies always operate within established political contexts as normative injuctions, determining what qualifies as intelligible sex, invoking and consolidating the reproductive constraints on sexuality, setting the prescriptive requirements whereby sexed or gendered bodies come into cultural intelligibility. Ontology is, thus, not a foundation, but a normative injunction that operates insidiously by installing itself into political discourse as its necessary ground. (203)

This study examines women’s reproductive health and the medicalization of women’s bodies by listening to women and validating “women’s ways of knowing.” This book contributes to a growing corpus of patient-centered public health literature by analyzing women’s reproductive health across the lifespan. The women interviewed in this book demand accurate information, including the risks and benefits of health care, and access to reproductive services and technologies. The analysis disrupts the nature/technology dualism and reconceptualizes health outside of the normative processes of menstruation, pregnancy, and childbirth. By talking with women, this study privileges women’s decision making about reproductive health and offers insight for how women’s partners, families, and health care providers can support them in this process.

# Bibliography

Adam, Hajo, and Adam D. Galinsky. 2012. "Enclothed Cognition." *Journal of Experimental Social Psychology*. doi:10.1016/j.jesp.2012.02.008.
Aengst, Jennifer, and Linda L. Layne. 2014. "The Need to Bleed? A Feminist Technology Assessment of Menstrual-Suppressing Birth Control Pills." In *Women, Science, and Technology: A Reader in Feminist Science Studies*, edited by Mary Wyer, Mary Barbercheck, Donna Cookmeyer, Hatice Ozturk, and Marta Wayne, 171–92. New York, NY: Routledge.
Aeschylus. 1989. *Eumenides*. In A. H. Sommerstein (Ed.), *Cambridge Greek and Latin Classics*. New York, NY: Cambridge University Press.
Agency for Healthcare Research and Quality (AHRQ). 2013. "U.S. Preventive Services Task Force. Preventive & Chronic Care Program: Improving Primary Care." U.S. Department of Health & Human Services. http://www.ahrq.gov/clinic/uspstfix.htm.
American Cancer Society (ACS). 2012. "Our History." http://www.cancer.org/aboutus/who-weare/our-history.
American College of Obstetricians and Gynecologists. 2013. "Planned Home Birth." *Committee Opinion* 117 (476): 425–28.
Armstrong, Natalie, and Elizabeth Murphy. 2008. "Weaving Meaning? An Exploration of the Interplay between Lay and Professional Understandings of Cervical Cancer Risk." *Social Science & Medicine* 67 (7): 1074–82.
Aschengrau, A, and G. R. Seague III. 2008. *Essentials of Epidemiology in Public Health*. Sudbury, MA: Jones & Bartlett Publishers.
Babrow, Austin S., and K. N. Kline. 2000. "From Reducing to Coping with Uncertainty: Reconceptualizing the Central Challenge in Breast Self-Exams." *Social Science & Medicine* 51 (12): 1805–16. doi:10.1016/S0277–9536(00)00112–X.
Babrow, Austin S., and Marifran Mattson. 2008. "Theorizing about Health Communication." In *Handbook of Health Communication*, edited by T. L. Thompson, A. Dorsey, K. I. Miller, and R. Parrott, 35–62. New York, NY: Routledge.
———. 2011. "Building Health Communication Theories in the 21st Century." In *The Routledge Handbook of Health Communication*, edited by Teresa L. Thompson, Roxanne Parrott, and Jon F. Nussbaum, Second, 18–35. New York, NY: Routledge.
Bachelard, G. 1994. *The Poetics of Space*. Boston, MA: Beacon Press.
Bailey, Lucy. 1999. "Refracted Selves? A Study of Changes in Self-Identity in the Transition to Motherhood." *Sociology* 33 (2): 335–52. doi:10.1177/S0038038599000206.
Baines, C. J. 2011. "Frank Words about Breast Screening." *Open Medicine* 5 (3): e134–36.
Barston, Suzanne. 2012. *Bottled Up: How the Way We Feed Babies Has Come to Define Motherhood, and Why It Shouldn't*. Berkeley: University of California Press.
Beauvoir, Simone de. 2011. *The Second Sex*. New York: Random House, Inc.

Becker, B. J., and S. J. Betstadt. 2013. "Patient Perception of Safety of Hormonal Contraception Compared to Pregnancy." Presented at the Annual Clinical Meeting of the American College of Obstetricians and Gynecologists, New Orleans, LA.

Benson, R. 1997. "The One with All the Jealousy." *Friends*. Burbank, CA: Warner Bros. Studios.

Benyo, Anna, Gretchen Borchelt, Karen Davenport, Kelli Garcia, Danielle Garrett, Stephanie Glover, Sharon Levin, Dania Palanker, Mara Gandal-Powers, and Courtney Ross. 2015. *State of Women's Coverage: Health Plan Violations of the Affordable Care Act*. Washington, D.C.: National Women's Law Center.

Benyo, Anna, Gretchen Borchelt, Karen Davenport, Danielle Garrett, Stephanie Glover, Sharon Levin, Dania Palanker, Mara Gandal-Powers, Courtney Ross, and Brandie Temple. 2015. *State of Birth Control Coverage: Health Plan Violations of the Affordable Care Act*. Washington, D.C.: National Women's Law Center.

Berg, B. L. 2009. *Qualitative Research Methods for the Social Sciences*. 7th ed. Boston: Allyn & Bacon.

Berger, Michele Tracy, and Kathleen Guidroz. 2010. *The Intersectional Approach: Transforming the Academy through Race, Class, and Gender*. Chapel Hill: University of North Carolina Press.

Bird, Chloe E., and Patricia P. Rieker. 2008. *Gender and Health: The Effects of Constrained Choices and Social Policies*. Boston, MA: Cambridge University Press.

Blasberg, D. 2011. "Georgina Chapman: Red-Carpet Royalty." *Harper's Bazaar*, April, 202–205 edition.

Blizzard, Deborah. 2007. *Looking Within: A Sociocultural Examination of Fetoscopy*. Boston, MA: MIT Press.

Blum, Linda M. 2000. *At the Breast: Ideologies of Breastfeeding and Motherhood in the Contemporary United States*. Boston, MA: Beacon Press.

Blundell, S. 2001. *Women in Ancient Greece*. Cambridge, MA: Harvard University Press.

Boonstra, H., V. Duran, V. Northington Gamble, P. Blumenthal, L. Dominguez, and C. Pies. 2000. "The 'Boom and Bust Phenomenon': The Hopes, Dreams, and Broken Promises of the Contraceptive Revolution." *Contraception* 61 (1): 9–25. doi:10.1016/S0010–7824(99)00121–3.

Boyle, A. U., U. M. Reddy, and H. J. Landy. 2013. "Primary Cesarean Delivery in the United States." *Obstetrics & Gynecology* 122 (1): 33–40.

Brehaut, Jamie C., Dafna E. Kohen, Rochelle E. Garner, Anton R. Miller, Lucyna M. Lach, Anne F. Klassen, and Peter L. Rosenbaum. 2009. "Health Among Caregivers of Children With Health Problems: Findings From a Canadian Population-Based Study." *Am J Public Health* 99 (7): 1254–62. doi: 10.2105/AJPH.2007.129817

Briones, Rowena, and Beth Sundstrom. 2013. "Reaching the Unreachable: How eHealth and Mobile Health Technologies Impact At-Risk Populations." In *Health Communication and Mass Media: An Integrated Approach to Policy and Practice*, edited by R. Ahmed and B. R. Bates, 133–50. Burlington, VT: Gower Publishing.

Bute, Jennifer J. 2009. "'Nobody Thinks Twice about Asking': Women with a Fertility Problem and Requests for Information." *Health Communication* 24 (8): 752–63. doi:10.1080/10410230903265920.

Bute, Jennifer J., and Robin E. Jensen. 2010. "Low-Income Women Describe Fertility-Related Expectations: Descriptive Norms, Injunctive Norms, and Behavior." *Health Communication* 25 (8): 681–91. doi:10.1080/10410236.2010.521909.

Butler, Judith. 2010. *Gender Trouble: Feminism and the Subversion of Identity*. New York, NY: Routledge.

Caiata-Zuffrey, M., and P. J. Schulz. 2012. "Physicians' Communicative Strategies in Interacting with Internet-Informed Patients: Results from a Qualitative Study." *Health Communication* 27 (7): 738–49. doi:10.1080/10410236.2011.636478.

Centers for Disease Control and Prevention (CDC). 1983. "Elevated Risk of Pelvic Inflammatory Disease among Women Using the Dalkon Shield." *Morbidity and Mortality Weekly Report* 32 (17): 221–22.

Centers for Disease Control and Prevention (CDC). 1999. "Ten Great Public Health Achievements—United States, 1900–1990." *Morbidity and Mortality Weekly Report* 48 (12): 241–43.

Chung, Heesu, Hyeyeon Lee, Dong-Seon Chang, Ho-Sun Kim, Hyejung Lee, Hi-Joon Park, and Younbyoung Chae. 2012. "Doctor's Attire Influences Perceived Empathy in the Patient–doctor Relationship." *Patient Education and Counseling*. doi:10.1016/j.pec.2012.02.017.

Cirksena, K., and L. Cuklanz. 1992. "Male Is to Female as ____ Is to ____: A Guided Tour of Five Feminist Frameworks for Communication Studies." In *Women Making Meaning: New Feminist Directions in Communication*, edited by L. F. Rakow. New York: Routledge.

Clark, E. A., and R. M. Smith. 2011. "Long-Term Maternal Morbidity Associated with Repeat Cesarean Delivery." *American Journal of Obstetrics and Gynecology* 205: S2–10.

Cline, Rebecca J. Welch. 2011. "Everyday Interpersonal Communication And Health." In *The Routledge Handbook of Health Communication*, edited by Teresa L. Thompson, Roxanne Parrott, and Jon F. Nussbaum, Second, 377–96. New York, NY: Routledge. http://www.routledge.com/books/details/9780415883153/.

———. 2008. "Everyday Interpersonal Communication and Health." In *Handbook of Health Communication*, 285–318. New York, NY: Routledge.

Colen, Cynthia G., and David M. Ramey. 2014. "Is Breast Truly Best? Estimating the Effects of Breastfeeding on Long-Term Child Health and Wellbeing in the United States Using Sibling Comparisons." *Social Science & Medicine* 109 (May): 55–65. doi:10.1016/j.socscimed.2014.01.027.

Collins English Dictionary. 2003. "Collins English Dictionary—Complete and Unabridged." Harper Collins Publishers.

Collins, Gail. 2009. *When Everything Changed: The Amazing Journey of American Women from 1960 to the Present*. New York, NY: Little, Brown and Company.

Cook, K., and C. Loomis. 2012. "The Impact of Choice and Control on Women's Childbirth Experiences." *The Journal of Perinatal Education* 21 (3): 158–68. doi:10.1891/1058–1243.21.3.158.

Cooper, M. 2011. "Reasons for Non-Attendance at Cervical Screening." *Nursing Standard* 25 (26): 41–46.

Corbin, Juliet, and Anselm Strauss. 2008. *Basics of Qualitative Research: Techniques and Procedures for Developing Grounded Theory*. 3rd ed. Thousand Oaks, CA: Sage Publications, Inc.

Cottrell, Erika K. Barth, Ngoc Wasson, Jesse Wagner, Elaine Graham, and Jeanne-Marie Guise. 2012. "Vaginal Birth After Cesarean: Developing and Prioritizing a Future Research Agenda." *Agency for Healthcare Research and Quality* Future Research Needs Paper No. 15. (AHRQ Publication No. 12-EHC072-EF). www.effectivehealthcare.ahrq.gov/reports/final.cfm.

Coutinho, Elsimar M., and Sheldon Jerome Segal. 1999. *Is Menstruation Obsolete?*. New York: Oxford University Press.

Covey, J. 2011. "The Effects of Absolute Risks, Relative Risks, Frequencies, and Probabilities on Decision Quality." *Journal of Health Communication* 16 (7): 788–801.

Croswell, Jennifer Miller, Barnett S. Kramer, Aimee R. Kreimer, Phil C. Prorok, Jian-Lun Xu, Stuart G. Baker, Richard Fagerstrom, et al. 2009. "Cumulative Incidence of False-Positive Results in Repeated, Multimodal Cancer Screening." *The Annals of Family Medicine* 7 (3): 212–22. doi:10.1370/afm.942.

Croswell, Jennifer M., David F. Ransohoff, and Barnett S. Kramer. 2010. "Principles of Cancer Screening: Lessons from History and Study Design Issues." *Seminars in Oncology* 37 (3): 202–15. doi:10.1053/j.seminoncol.2010.05.006.

Daniels, Kimberly, William D. Mosher, and Jo Jones. 2013. *Contraceptive Methods Women Have Ever Used: United States, 1982–2010*. 62. National Health Statistics Reports (NHSR). U.S. Department of Health and Human Services.

Davis, Angela Y. 1981. *Women, Race, & Class*. New York, NY: Random House, Inc.

Davis-Floyd, Robbie. 2003. *Birth as an American Rite of Passage*. Berkeley and Los Angeles: University of California Press.

Dencker, A., C. Taft, L. Bergqvist, H. Lilja, and M. Berg. 2010. "Childbirth Experience Questionnaire (CEQ): Development and Evaluation of a Multidimensional Instrument." *BMC Pregnancy and Childbirth* 10 (1). doi:10.1186/1471–2393–10–81.

Department of Health and Human Services. 2014. *Health Insurance Marketplace: Summary Enrollment Report for the Initial Annual Open Enrollment Period.* ASPE Issue Brief. Office of the Assistant Secretary for Planning and Evaluation. http://aspe.hhs.gov.

Drolet, M., M. Brisson, E. Maunsell, E. L. Franco, F. Coutlee, A. Ferenczy, J. A. Mansi, and et al. 2012. "The Psychosocial Impact of an Abnormal Cervical Smear Result." *Psycho-Oncology* 21 (10): 1071–81.

Dutta, Mohan J., and Ambar Basu. 2011. "Culture, Communication, and Health: A Guiding Framework." In *The Routledge Handbook of Health Communication*, edited by Teresa L. Thompson, Roxanne Parrott, and Jon F. Nussbaum, Second, 320–34. New York, NY: Routledge. http://www.routledge.com/books/details/9780415883153/.

Edelman, Alison, Elizabeth Micks, Maria F. Gallo, Jeffrey T. Jensen, and David A. Grimes. 2014. "Continuous or Extended Cycle vs. Cyclic Use of Combined Hormonal Contraceptives for Contraception." *The Cochrane Database of Systematic Reviews* 7: CD004695. doi:10.1002/14651858.CD004695.pub3.

Ehrenreich, Barbara, and Deirdre English. 2005. *For Her Own Good: Two Centuries of the Experts Advice to Women*. New York, NY: Anchor Books.

———. 2010. *Witches, Midwives, and Nurses: A History of Women Healers*. New York City: The Feminist Press at CUNY.

Eisenberg, David, Colleen McNicholas, and Jeffrey F. Peipert. 2013. "Cost as a Barrier to Long-Acting Reversible Contraceptive (LARC) Use in Adolescents." *Journal of Adolescent Health* 52 (4, Supplement): S59–63. doi:10.1016/j.jadohealth.2013.01.012.

Ettorre, E. 2000. "Reproductive Genetics, Gender and the Body: 'Please Doctor, May I Have a Normal Baby.'" *Sociology* 34 (3): 403–20. doi:10.1177/S0038038500000262.

Finer, Lawrence B., Jenna Jerman, and Megan L. Kavanaugh. 2012. "Changes in Use of Long-Acting Contraceptive Methods in the United States, 2007–2009." *Fertility and Sterility* 98 (4): 893–97. doi:10.1016/j.fertnstert.2012.06.027.

Fisher, C., Y. Hauck, S. Bayes, and J. Byrne. 2012. "Participant Experiences of Mindfulness-Based Childbirth Education: A Qualitative Study." *BMC Pregnancy and Childbirth* 12 (1). doi:10.1186/1471–2393–12–126.

Foley, Dolores. 1999. "Organizing for Social Change and Policy Reform: Lessons from the International Planned Parenthood Federation." *International Journal of Organization Theory & Behavior* 2 (1/2): 89.

Foster, Diana Greene, Daniel Grossman, David K. Turok, Jeffrey F. Peipert, Linda Prine, Courtney A. Schreiber, Andrea V. Jackson, Rana E. Barar, and Eleanor Bimla Schwarz. 2014. "Interest in and Experience with IUD Self-Removal." *Contraception* 90 (1): 54–59. doi:10.1016/j.contraception.2014.01.025.

Foucault, M. 1978. *The History of Sexuality: An Introduction*. Vol. Vintage Books Edition. 1–3 vols. New York, NY: Random House, Inc.

Fox, S. A., J. Heritage, S. E. Stockdale, S. M. Asch, N. Duan, and S. P. Reise. 2009. "Cancer Screening Adherence: Does Physician-Patient Communication Matter?" *Patient Education and Counseling* 75 (2): 178–84.

Friedan, Betty. 2001. *The Feminine Mystique*. New York, NY: W. W. Norton & Company.

Friedman, E.A. 1955. "Primigravid Labor; A Graphicostatistical Analysis." *Obstetrics & Gynecology* 6 (6): 567–89.

Frost, Jennifer J., Adam Sonfield, Mia R. Zolna, and Lawrence B. Finer. 2014. "Return on Investment: A Fuller Assessment of the Benefits and Cost Savings of the US Publicly Funded Family Planning Program." *The Milbank Quarterly*, 1–54.

Gavin, L., S. Moskosky, and M. Carter. 2014. "Providing Quality Family Planning Services: Recommendations of CDC and the U.S. Office of Population Affairs." *Morbidity and Mortality Weekly Report* 63 (4): 1–54.

Giordano, L., V. Stefanini, C. Senore, A. Frigerio, R. Castagno, V. Marra, and N. Segnan. 2012. "The Impact of Different Communication and Organizational Strategies on Mammography Screening Uptake in Women Aged 40–45 Years." *European Journal of Public Health* 22 (3): 413–18.

Gladwell, Malcolm. 2000. "John Rock's Error." *The New Yorker*. March 6. http://www.newyorker.com/magazine/2000/03/13/john-rocks-error-2.

Glaser, Barney G., and Anselm L Strauss. 1967. *The Discovery of Grounded Theory: Strategies for Qualitative Research*. Chicago: Aldine.

Gold, Katherine J., Martha E. Boggs, Emeline Mugisha, and Christie Lancaster Palladino. 2012. "Internet Message Boards for Pregnancy Loss: Who's On-Line and Why?" *Women's Health Issues* 22 (1): e67–72. doi:10.1016/j.whi.2011.07.006.

Gordon, Lisa. 1997. "The Struggle for Reproductive Freedom." In *Controlling Reproduction: An American History*, edited by Andrea Tone, 147–55. Wilmington: Scholarly Resources.

Gordis, L. 2008. Epidemiology. Philadelphia, PA: Elsevier Health Sciences.

Gøtzsche, P. C., and M. Nielsen. 2011. "Screening for Breast Cancer with Mammography." *Cochrane Database of Systematic Reviews (Online)*, no. 1. doi:10.1002/14651858.CD001877.pub4.

Gould, J., B. Danielson, L. Korst, R. Phibbs, K. Chance, and E. K. Main. 2004. "Cesarean Delivery Rate and Neonatal Morbidity in a Low-Risk Population" 104: 11–19.

Gramsci, A. 1971. *Selections from the Prison Notebooks of Antonio Gramsci*. Q. Hoare and G.N. Smith. New York: International Publishers.

Greene, M., S. Joshi, and O. Robles. 2012. *By Choice, Not by Chance: Family Planning, Human Rights and Development*. The State of World Population 2012. United Nations Population Fund.

*Griswold v. Connecticut*. 1965. The Supreme Court of the United States.

Grossman, Daniel, Kate Grindlay, Rick Li, Joseph E. Potter, James Trussell, and Kelly Blanchard. 2013. "Interest in Over-the-Counter Access to Oral Contraceptives Among Women in the United States." *Contraception* 88 (4): 544–52. doi:10.1016/j.contraception.2013.04.005.

Guest, Greg, and Kathleen M. MacQueen, eds. 2008. *Handbook for Team-Based Qualitative Research*. Lanham, MD: Rowman Altamira.

Gurrieri, Lauren, Josephine Previte, and Jan Brace-Govan. 2013. "Women's Bodies as Sites of Control: Inadvertent Stigma and Exclusion in Social Marketing." *Journal of Macromarketing* 33 (2): 128–43. doi:10.1177/0276146712469971.

Guttmacher Institute. 2014. "Contraceptive Use in the United States." Guttmacher Institute. http://www.guttmacher.org/pubs/fb_contr_use.html#2.

———. 2015. *Trends in the States: First Quarter 2015*. News in Context. Washington, D.C.: Media Center.

Hafslund, B., and M. W. Nortvedt. 2009. "Mammography Screening from the Perspective of Quality of Life: A Review of the Literature." *Scandanavian Journal of Caring Science* 23 (3): 539–48.

Haggstrom, D. A., and M. M. Schapira. 2006. "Black-White Differences in Risk Perception of Breast Cancer Survival and Screening Mammography Benefit." *Journal of General Internal Medicine (JGIM)* 21 (4): 371–77.

Haines, H. M., C. Rubertsson, J. F. Pallant, and I. Hildingsson. 2012. "The Influence of Women's Fear, Attitudes and Beliefs of Childbirth on Mode and Experience of Birth." *BMC Pregnancy and Childbirth* 12 (1). doi:10.1186/1471–2393–12–55.

Hannaford, P. C., L. Iverson, T. V. Macfarlane, A. M. Elliot, V. Angus, and A. J. Lee. 2010. "Mortality Among Contraceptive Pill Users: Cohort Evidence from Royal College of General Practitioners' Oral Contraception Study." *British Medical Journal* 340 (c927). doi:10.1136/bmj.c927.

Hanoch, Y. 2004. "Improving Doctor-Patient Understanding of Probability in Communicating Cancer-Screening Test Findings." *Journal of Health Communication* 9 (4): 327–35.

Haraway, Donna Jeanne. 2004. *The Haraway Reader*. New York, NY: Routledge.

Harding, S. 2004. *The Feminist Standpoint Theory Reader: Intellectual and Political Controversies*. New York, NY: Routledge.

Hawkesworth, Mary. 2006. *Feminist Inquiry: From Political Conviction to Methodological Innovation*. New Brunswick, NJ: Rutgers University Press.

Health Resources and Services Administration. 2014. "Women's Preventive Services Guidelines." *U.S. Department of Health and Human Services*. http://www.hrsa.gov/womensguidelines/.

HealthyPeople.gov. 2014. "Healthy People 2020." http://www.healthypeople.gov/2020/topicsobjectives2020/default.aspx.

Hersch, J., J. Jansen, A. Barratt, L. Irwig, N. Houssami, K. Howard, and K. McCaffery. 2013. "Women's Views on Overdiagnosis in Breast Cancer Screening: A Qualitative Study." *BMJ: British Medical Journal* 346: f158–f158. doi:10.1136/bmj.f158.

Hesse-Biber, Sharlene Nagy, and Patricia Leavy. 2007. *Feminist Research Practice: A Primer*. SAGE.

Hidaka, R., and L.C. Callister. 2012. "Giving Birth with Epidural Analgesia: The Experience of First-Time Mothers." *The Journal of Perinatal Education* 21 (1): 24–35. doi:10.1891/1058–1243.21.1.24.

Hillard, Paula. 2014. "Menstrual Suppression: Current Perspectives." *International Journal of Women's Health*, June, 631. doi:10.2147/IJWH.S46680.

Hitchcock, Christine, and Ingrid Johnston-Robledo. 2007. *Society for Menstrual Cycle Research Calls for More Research on Long-term Effects of Cycle-Stopping: Contraceptives: Menstruation Is Not A Disease*. Vancouver, British Columbia, Canada: Society for Menstrual Cycle Research. http://menstruationresearch.org/wp-content/uploads/2009/07/SMCRposition06082007.pdf.

Holmes-Royner, M., and S. Charles. 2003. "The Mammography Screening Controversy: Who and What Is Heard in the Press?" *Patient Education & Counseling* 51 (1): 75.

hooks, b. 1984. *Feminist Theory: From Margin to Center*. Boston, MA: South End Press.

Hubbard, R. A., D. L. Miglioretti, and R. A. Smith. 2010. "Modeling the Cumulative Risk of a False-Positive Screening Test." *Statistical Methods in Medical Research* 19 (5): 429–49. doi:10.1177/0962280209359842.

Hunter, William. 1774. *The Anatomy of the Human Gravid Uterus*. Copperplate engraving. National Library of Medicine. National Institutes of Health. http://www.nlm.nih.gov/dreamanatomy/da_g_II-B-1.html.

Jaffe, Frederick S. 1973. "Some Policy and Program Implications of 'Contraceptive Failure in the United States.'" *Family Planning Perspectives* 5 (3): 143–44.

Jensen, J. D., N. Carcioppolo, A. J. King, J. K. Bernat, L. Davis, R. Yale, and J. Smith. 2011. "Including Limitation in News Coverage of Cancer Research: Effects of News Hedging on Fatalism, Medical Skepticism, Patient Trust, and Backlash." *Journal of Health Communication* 16 (5): 486–503. doi:10.1080/10810730.2010.546491.

Jensen, J. T., and James Trussell. 2012. "Communicating Risk: Does Scientific Debate Compromise Safety?" *Contraception* 86 (4): 327–29. doi:10.1016/j.contraception.2012.06.010.

Jones, Jo, William Mosher, and Kimberly Daniels. 2012. *Current Contraceptive Use in the United States, 2006–2010, and Changes in Patterns of Use Since 1995*. National Health Statistics Reports (NHSR) 60. Hyattsville, MD: National Center for Health Statistics.

Jones, R. K. 2011. *Beyond Birth Control: The Overlooked Benefits of Oral Contraceptive Pills*. New York: Guttmacher Institute.

Jones, R. K., and J. Dreweke. 2011. *Countering Conventional Wisdom: New Evidence on Religion and Contraceptive Use*. New York: Guttmacher Institute.

Kaiser Family Foundation. 2006. *Rhode Island: Percentage of Mothers Beginning Prenatal Care in the First Trimester by Race/ethnicity*. statehealthfacts.org.

———. 2008a. *Rhode Island Births*. statehealthfacts.org.

———. 2008b. *Rhode Island: Preterm Births as a Percent of All Births by Race/ethnicity*. statehealthfacts.org.

Kalager, M., H-O Adami, M. Bretthauer, and R. M. Tamimi. 2012. "Overdiagnosis of Invasive Breast Cancer Due to Mammography Screening: Results from the Norwegian Screening Program." *Annals of Internal Medicine* 156 (7): 491 – W – 161.

Kaufman, T. 2007. "Evolution of a Birth Plan." *Journal of Perinatal Education* 16 (3): 47–52. doi:10.1624/105812407X217985.

Keen, John D., and James E. Keen. 2009. "What Is the Point: Will Screening Mammography Save My Life?" *BMC Medical Informatics and Decision Making* 9 (1): 18. doi:10.1186/1472–6947–9–18.

Kline, Kimberly N. 2011. "Popular Media and Health: Images and Effects." In *The Routledge Handbook of Health Communication*, edited by Teresa L. Thompson, Roxanne Parrott, and Jon F. Nussbaum, Second, 252–67. New York: Routledge. http://www.routledge.com/books/details/9780415883153/.

———. 2006. "A Decade of Research on Health Content in the Media: The Focus on Health Challenges and Sociocultural Context and Attendant Informational and Ideological Problems." *Journal of Health Communication* 11 (1): 43–59. doi:10.1080/10810730500461067.

———. 2008. "Popular Media and Health: Images, Effects, and Institutions." In *Handbook of Health Communication*, edited by T. L. Thompson, A. Dorsey, K.I. Miller, and R. Parrott, 557–82. Mahwah, New Jersey: Lawrence Erlbaum Associates, Inc.

Koehn, M. 2008. "Contemporary Women's Perceptions of Childbirth Education." *Journal of Perinatal Education* 17 (1): 11–18. doi:10.1624/105812408X267916.

Kost, K., J. D. Forrest, and S. Harlap. 1991. "Comparing the Health Risks and Benefits of Contraceptive Choices." *Family Planning Perspectives* 23 (2): 54–61.

Lakehomer, Hannah, Paul F. Kaplan, David G. Wozniak, and Christopher T. Minson. 2013. "Characteristics of Scheduled Bleeding Manipulation with Combined Hormonal Contraception in University Students." *Contraception* 88 (3): 426–30. doi:10.1016/j.contraception.2012.12.012.

Lather, P. 1991. *Getting Smart: Feminist Research and Pedagogy With/in the Postmodern*. New York: Routledge.

Leavitt, Judith Walzer. 1997. "'Science' Enters the Birthing Room: Obstetrics in America since the Eighteenth Century." In *Controlling Reproduction: An American History*, edited by Andrea Tone, 33–58. Wilmington, DE: Scholarly Resources.

Lefkowitz, Mary R., and Maureen B. Fant. 2005. *Women's Life in Greece and Rome: A Source Book in Translation*. JHU Press.

Letherby, Gayle. 2003. *Feminist Research in Theory and Practice*. McGraw-Hill International.

Lewis, Rashonda M., J. Nikki McKoy, Jeffrey C. Andrews, Rebecca N. Jerome, Frances E. Likis, Tanya S. Surawicz, Stephaine H. Walker, and Katherine E. Hartmann. 2012. "Future Research Needs for Strategies To Reduce Cesarean Birth in Low-Risk Women." *Agency for Healthcare Research and Quality* Future Research Needs Paper No. 22 (.) AHRQ Publication No. 12(13)– EHC131–EF). www.effectivehealthcare.ahrq.gov/reports/final.cfm.

Lindlof, Thomas R., and Bryan C. Taylor. 2010. *Qualitative Communication Research Methods*. SAGE.

Loudon, Irvine. 2000. "Maternal Mortality in the Past and Its Relevance to Developing Countries Today." *The American Journal of Clinical Nutrition* 72 (1): 241s – 246s.

Lyerly, A. D., L. M. Mitchell, E. M. Armstrong, L. H. Harris, R. Kukla, M. Kuppermann, and M. O. Little. 2009. "RISK and the Pregnant Body." *The Hastings Center Report* 39 (6).

MacDorman, M. F., T. J. Mathews, and E. Declercq. 2012. *Home Births in the United States 1990–2009*. NCHS data brief 84. Hyattsville, MD: National Center for Health Statistics.

MacGeorge, Erina L., and Kristi Wilkum. 2012. "Predicting Comforting Quality in the Context of Miscarriage." *Communication Reports* 25 (2): 62–74. doi:10.1080/08934215.2012.719463.

Malacrida, C., and T. Boulton. 2012. "Women's Perceptions of Childbirth 'Choices' Competing Discourses of Motherhood, Sexuality, and Selflessness." *Gender & Society* 26 (5): 748–72. doi:10.1177/0891243212452630.

Mansour, Diana, Kristina Gemzell-Danielsson, Pirjo Inki, and Jeffrey T. Jensen. 2011. "Fertility After Discontinuation of Contraception: A Comprehensive Review of the Literature." *Contraception* 84 (5): 465–77. doi:10.1016/j.contraception.2011.04.002.

Martin, Emily. 2001. *The Woman in the Body: A Cultural Analysis of Reproduction*. Boston: Beacon Press.

Meguerditchian, A.-N., D. Dauphinee, N. Girard, T. Eguale, K. Riedel, A. Jacques, and R. Tamblyn. 2012. "Do Physician Communication Skills Influence Screening Mammography Utilization?" *BMC Health Services Research* 12 (1): 219–26.

Merriam-Webster. 2004. *Merriam-Webster's Collegiate Dictionary: Eleventh Edition*. United States of America: Merriam-Webster, Inc.

Miles, M. B., and A. M. Huberman. 1994. *Qualitative Data Analysis: An Expanded Sourcebook*. Second edition. Thousand Oaks: Sage Publications, Inc.

Minh-ha, T. T. 1989. *Women, Native, Other: Writing Postcoloniality and Feminism*. Indianapolis: Indiana University Press.

Moran, D. 2000. *Introduction to Phenomenology*. New York: Routledge.

Morris, Madeleine. 2014. *Guilt-Free Bottle Feeding: Why Your Formula-Fed Baby Can Be Happy, Healthy and Smart*. Devon, UK: White Ladder Press.

Morton, C. H., and C. Hsu. 2007. "Contemporary Dilemmas in American Childbirth Education: Findings from a Comparative Ethnographic Study." *Journal of Perinatal Education* 16 (4): 25–37. doi:10.1624/105812407X245614.

Mosher, W. D., and J. Jones. 2010. "Use of Contraception in the United States: 1982–2008. National Center for Health Statistics." *Vital Health Statistics* 23 (29).

Moyer, V. A. 2012a. "Screening for Cervical Cancer: U.S. Preventive Services Task Force Recommendation Statement." *Annals of Internal Medicine*, W312, 156 (12): 880–91. doi:10.7326/0003–4819–156–12–201206190–00424.

———. 2012b. "Screening for Ovarian Cancer: U.S. Preventive Services Task Force Reaffirmation Recommendation Statement." *Annals of Internal Medicine* 157 (12): 900–904. doi:10.7326/0003–4819–157–11–201212040–00539.

Murphy, Elaine. 2004. "Diffusion of Innovations: Family Planning in Developing Countries." *Journal of Health Communication* 9 (January): 123–29. doi:10.1080/10810730490271566.

Nagy, Gyula Richárd, Balázs Győrffy, Bálint Nagy, and János Rigó Jr. 2013. "Lower Risk for Down Syndrome Associated with Longer Oral Contraceptive Use: A Case-control Study of Women of Advanced Maternal Age Presenting for Prenatal Diagnosis." *Contraception* 87 (4): 455–58. doi:10.1016/j.contraception.2012.08.040.

Nekhlyudov, L., and C. H. Braddock III. 2009. "An Approach to Enhance Communication about Screening Mammography in Primary Care." *Journal of Women's Health (15409996)* 18 (9): 1403–12.

Nolen, B. M., and A. E. Lokshin. 2012. "Protein Biomarkers of Ovarian Cancer: The Forest and the Trees." *Future Oncology* 8 (1): 55–71. doi:10.2217/fon.11.135.

O'Grady, Helen. 2004. "An Ethics of the Self." In *Feminism and the Final Foucault*, edited by Dianna Taylor and Karen Vintges, 91–117. Chicago, IL: University of Illinois Press.

Olsen, Ole, and Jette A. Clausen. 1996. "Planned Hospital Birth versus Planned Home Birth." In *Cochrane Database of Systematic Reviews*. Hoboken, NJ: John Wiley & Sons, Ltd. http://onlinelibrary.wiley.com.nuncio.cofc.edu/doi/10.1002/14651858.CD000352.pub2/abstract.

Osotimehin, Babatunde. 2012. *Foreward. In by Choice, Not by Chance: Family Planning, Human Rights and Development*. The State of World Population 2012. United Nations Population Fund.

Parrott, Roxanne, and Matthew W. Kreuter. 2011. "Multidisciplinary, Interdisciplinary, and Transdisciplinary Approaches to Health Communication: Where Do We Draw the Line?" In *The Routledge Handbook of Health Communication*, edited by Teresa L. Thompson, Roxanne Parrott, and Jon F. Nussbaum, Second, 3–17. New York, NY: Routledge. http://www.routledge.com/books/details/9780415883153/.

Pear, Robert. 2015. "House G.O.P. Again Votes to Repeal Health Care Law." *The New York Times*, February 3. http://www.nytimes.com/2015/02/04/us/politics/house-gop-again-votes-to-repeal-health-care-law.html.

Peel, E. 2010. "Pregnancy Loss in Lesbian and Bisexual Women: An Online Survey of Experiences." *Human Reproduction* 25 (3): 721–27. doi:10.1093/humrep/dep441.

Peipert, Jeffrey F., Qiuhong Zhao, Laura Meints, Benjamin J. Peipert, Colleen A. Redding, and Jenifer E. Allsworth. 2011. "Adherence to Dual Method Contraceptive Use." *Contraception* 84 (3): 252–58. doi:10.1016/j.contraception.2011.01.023.

Picavet, Charles. 2014. "Skipping the Pill-Free Interval: Data from a Dutch National Sample." *Contraception* 89 (1): 28–30. doi:10.1016/j.contraception.2013.09.005.

Plutynski, A. 2012. "Ethical Issues in Cancer Screening and Prevention." *Journal of Medicine & Philosophy* 37 (3): 310–23.

Politi, M. C., M. A. Clark, M. L. Rogers, K. McGarry, and C. N. Sciamanna. 2008. "Patient-Provider Communication and Cancer Screening among Unmarried Women." *Patient Education & Counseling* 73 (2): 251–55.

Pollock, D. 1999. *Telling Bodies Performing Birth: Everyday Narratives of Childbirth*. New York: Columbia University Press.

Rangel, Charles. 2010. *Patient Protection and Affordable Care Act*.

Reagan, Leslie J. 2012. *Dangerous Pregnancies: Mothers, Disabilities, and Abortion in Modern America*. Berkeley and Los Angeles, California: University of California Press.

Reinharz, S. 1992. *Feminist Methods in Social Research*. New York, NY: Oxford University Press.

Roberts, Dorothy. 1997. *Killing the Black Body: Race, Reproduction, and the Meaning of Liberty*. New York, NY: Pantheon Books.

Rogers, Everett M., Peter W. Vaughan, Ramadhan M.A. Swalehe, Nagesh Rao, Peer Svenkerud, and Suruchi Sood. 1999. "Effects of an Entertainment-Education Radio Soap Opera on Family Planning Behavior in Tanzania." *Studies in Family Planning* 30 (3): 193–211.

Romano, A. M. 2007. "A Changing Landscape: Implications of Pregnant Women's Internet Use for Childbirth Educators." *Journal of Perinatal Education* 16 (4): 18–24. doi:10.1624/105812407X244903.

Romano, A. M., H. Gerber, and D. Andrews. 2010. "Social Media, Power, and the Future of VBAC." *Journal of Perinatal Education* 19 (3): 43–52. doi:10.1624/105812410X514431.

Romano, A. M., and J. A. Lothian. 2008. "Promoting, Protecting, and Supporting Normal Birth: A Look at the Evidence." *Journal of Obstetric, Gynecologic, & Neonatal Nursing* 37 (1): 94–105. doi:10.1111/j.1552–6909.2007.00210.x.

Rooks, Judith. 1999. *Midwifery and Childbirth in America*. Philadelphia: Temple University Press.

Rose, Sally B., Annette J. Cooper, Naomi K. Baker, and Beverley Lawton. 2011. "Attitudes Toward Long-Acting Reversible Contraception Among Young Women Seeking Abortion." *Journal of Women's Health (15409996)* 20 (11): 1729–35. doi:10.1089/jwh.2010.2658.

Rubin, Herbert J., and Irene Rubin. 2012. *Qualitative Interviewing: The Art of Hearing Data*. Third. Thousand Oaks: SAGE.

Sanger, Margaret. 1919. "Birth Control and Racial Betterment." *The Birth Control Review*, 11–12.

Satina, B., and F. Hultgren. 2001. "The Absent Body of Girls Made Visible: Embodiment as the Focus in Education." *Studies in Philosophy & Education* 20 (6): 521–34.

Sawaya, G. F. 2009. "Cervical-Cancer Screening—New Guidelines and the Balance between Benefits and Harms." *New England Journal of Medicine* 361 (26): 2503–5. doi:10.1056/NEJMp0911380.

Scherer, C. W., and N. K. Juanillo Jr. 2008. "The Continuing Challenge of Community Health Risk Management and Communication." In *Handbook of Health Communication*, 221–39. New York, NY: Routledge.

Schneider, M-J. 2010. *Introduction to Public Health*. Sudbury, MA: Jones & Bartlett Publishers.

Schwartz, John. 2014. "Between the Lines of the Contraception Decision." *The New York Times*, June 30. http://www.nytimes.com/interactive/2014/06/30/us/annotated-supreme-court-hobby-lobby-contraception-decision.html.

Secura, Gina M., Jenifer E. Allsworth, Tessa Madden, Jennifer L. Mullersman, and Jeffrey F. Peipert. 2011. "The Contraceptive CHOICE Project: Reducing Barriers to Long-Acting Reversible Contraception." *American Journal of Obstetrics and Gynecology* 203 (2): 115.e1–115.e7. doi:10.1016/j.ajog.2010.04.017.

Secura, Gina M., Tessa Madden, Colleen McNicholas, Jennifer Mullersman, Christina M. Buckel, Qiuhong Zhao, and Jeffrey F. Peipert. 2014. "Provision of No-Cost, Long-Acting Contraception and Teenage Pregnancy." *New England Journal of Medicine* 371 (14): 1316–23. doi:10.1056/NEJMoa1400506.

Sevón, Eija. 2005. "Timing Motherhood: Experiencing and Narrating the Choice to Become a Mother." *Feminism & Psychology* 15 (4): 461–82. doi:10.1177/0959–353505057619.

Sharf, Barbara F., Lynn M. Harter, Jill Yamasaki, and Paul Haidet. 2011. "Narrative Turns Epic: Continuing Developments in Health Narrative Scholarship." In *The Routledge Handbook of Health Communication*, edited by Teresa L. Thompson, Roxanne Parrott, and Jon F. Nussbaum, Second, 36–51. New York, NY: Routledge. http://www.routledge.com/books/details/9780415883153/.

Sharf, Barbara F., and M.L. Vanderford. 2008. "Social Narratives and the Construction of Health." In *Beyond These Walls: Readings in Health Communication*, edited by L. C. Lederman, 24–46. New York: Oxford University Press.

Siegemund, Justine. 2005. *The Court Midwife*. Translated by Lynne Tatlock. Chicago: University Of Chicago Press.

Silverman, D., and A. Marvasti. 2008. *Doing Qualitative Research: A Comprehensive Guide*. Thousand Oaks: Sage Publications, Inc.

Sitruk-Ware, Regine, Anita Nath, and Daniel R. Mishell. 2013. "Contraception Technology: Past, Present and Future." *Contraception* 87 (3): 319–30. doi:10.1016/j.contraception.2012.08.002.

Smith, B. 1988. "Between a Rock and a Hard Place: Relationships Between Black and Jewish Women." In *Yours in Struggle: Three Feminist Perspectives on Anti-Semitism and Racism*, edited by E. Bulkin, M. B. Pratt, and B. Smith, 65–88. Ithaca, New York: Firebrand Books.

Smith, D. E. 2004. "Women's Perspective as a Radical Critique of Sociology." In *The Feminist Standpoint Theory Reader: Intellectual and Political Controversies*, edited by S. Harding, 21–34. New York: Routledge.

Smith, Susan L. 1995. *Sick and Tired of Being Sick and Tired: Black Women's Health Activism in America, 1890–1950*. Philadelphia: University of Pennsylvania Press.

Sobel, Laurie, Alina Salganicoff, and Nisha Kurani. 2015. "Coverage of Contraceptive Services: A Review of Health Insurance Plans in Five States." April 16. http://kff.org/private-insurance/report/coverage-of-contraceptive-services-a-review-of-health-insurance-plans-in-five-states/.

Song, F. W., J. E. West, L. Lundy, and N. S. Dahmen. 2012. "Women, Pregnancy, and Health Information Online: The Making of Informed Patients and Ideal Mothers." *Gender & Society* 26 (5): 773–98. doi:10.1177/0891243212446336.

Spong, C. Y., V. Berghella, K. D. Wenstrom, B. M. Mercer, and G. R. Saade. 2012. "Preventing the First Cesarean Delivery: Summary of the Joint Eunice Kennedy Shriver National Institute of Child Health and Human Development, Society for Maternal-Fetal Medicine, and American College of Obstetricians and Gynecologists Workshop." *Obstetrics & Gynecology* 120 (5): 1181–93.

Squiers, L. B., D. J. Holden, S. E. Dolina, A. E. Kim, C. M. Bann, and J. M. Renaud. 2011. "The Public's Response to the U.S. Preventive Services Task Force's 2009 Recommendations on Mammography Screening." *American Journal of Preventive Medicine* 40 (5): 497–504.

Stern, Lisa F., Hannah R. Simons, Julia E. Kohn, Elie J. Debevec, Johanna M. Morfesis, and Ashlesha A. Patel. 2015. "Differences in Contraceptive Use between Family Planning Providers and the U.S. Population: Results of a Nationwide Survey." *Contraception*, February. doi:10.1016/j.contraception.2015.02.005.

Strassmann, Beverly I. 1999. "Menstrual Cycling and Breast Cancer: An Evolutionary Perspective." *Journal of Women's Health* 8 (2): 193–202. doi:10.1089/jwh.1999.8.193.

Sundstrom, Beth. 2012. "Fifty Years on 'The Pill': A Qualitative Analysis of Nondaily Contraceptive Options." *Contraception* 86 (1): 4–11. doi:10.1016/j.contraception.2011.10.016.

———. 2013. "(Re)Writing the Body: A Prosumption Analysis of Pregnancy." *Journal of Social Marketing* 3 (2): 127–43. doi:10.1108/JSOCM-08-2011-0044.

———. 2014. "Breaking Women's Health Taboos Integrating Diffusion of Innovations Theory With Social Marketing." *Social Marketing Quarterly* 20 (2): 87–102. doi:10.1177/1524500414525774.

Sundstrom, Beth, D. Billings, I. Walters, L. McClorin, and K. Zenger. 2014. "Choose Well: Health Communication Strategies to Increase Awareness and Uptake of Highly-Effective Contraceptive Methods Among Young Women." *Contraception* 90 (2): 199–200.

Sundstrom, Beth, C. Szabo, and A. Dempsey. 2014. "A Qualitative Study of the Influence of Trust in the Health Care System on Postpartum Contraceptive Choice." *Contraception* 90 (3): 322.

Takeshita, Chikako. 2012. *The Global Biopolitics of the IUD: How Science Constructs Contraceptive Users and Women's Bodies*. Boston: MIT Press.

———. 2014. "The Need to Bleed? A Feminist Technology Assessment of Menstrual-Suppressing Birth Control Pills." In *Women, Science, and Technology: A Reader in Feminist Science Studies*, edited by Mary Wyer, Mary Barbercheck, Donna Cookmeyer, Hatice Ozturk, and Marta Wayne, 242–71. New York, NY: Routledge.

The American Heritage Dictionary. 2014. *The American Heritage (R) Dictionary of the English Language*. 4th ed. Houghton Mifflin Company.

Thornton, H., A. Edwards, and M. Baum. 2003. "Women Need Better Information about Routine Mammography." *BMJ: British Medical Journal (International Edition)* 327 (406): 101.

Tindall, Natalie T. J., and Jennifer Vardeman-Winter. 2011. "Complications in Segmenting Campaign Publics: Women of Color Explain Their Problems, Involvement, and Constraints in Reading Heart Disease Communication." *Howard Journal of Communications* 22 (3): 280–301. doi:10.1080/10646175.2011.590407.

Tone, Andrea. 1997. "Introduction." In *Controlling Reproduction: An American History*, edited by Andrea Tone, xiii–xxii. Wilmington, Del: Scholarly Resources.

———. 2002. *Devices & Desires: A History of Contraceptives in America*. Macmillan.

Truog, R. D. 2009. "Screening Mammography and the 'R' Word." *New England Journal of Medicine* 361 (26): 2501–3. doi:10.1056/NEJMp0911447.

Truss, A., R. Marshall, and C. Blair-Stevens. 2010. "A History of Social Marketing." In *Social Marketing and Public Health: Theory and Practice*, edited by J. French, C. Blair-Stevens, D. McVey, and R. Merritt. New York: Oxford University Press.

Trussell, James, Elizabeth G. Raymond, and Kelly Cleland. 2013. *Emergency Contraception: A Last Chance to Prevent Unintended Pregnancy*. Princeton, NJ: Princeton University Press. http://ec.princeton.edu/questions/ec-review.pdf.

Turner, Monique Mitchell, Christine Skubisz, and Jill Rimal. 2011. "Theory and Practice in Risk Communication: A Review of the Literature and Visions for the Future." In *The Routledge Handbook of Health Communication*, edited by Teresa L. Thompson, Roxanne Parrott, and Jon F. Nussbaum, Second, 146–64. New York, NY: Routledge. http://www.routledge.com/books/details/9780415883153/.

Upadhyay, U. D. 2005. *New Contraceptive Choices*. Population Reports No. 19. Series M. Baltimore, MD: The Johns Hopkins Bloomberg School of Public Health.

U.S. Census Bureau. 2010a. *Age Groups and Sex*. 2010 Census. Rhode Island. http://factfinder2.census.gov/faces/tableservices/jsf/pages/productview.xhtml?pid=DEC_10_SF1_QTP1&prodType=table.

———. 2010b. *Profile of General Population and Housing Characteristics*. 2010 Census. Rhode Island. http://factfinder2.census.gov/faces/tableservices/jsf/pages/productview.xhtml?pid=DEC_10_DP_DPDP1&prodType=table.

———. 2013. Educational Attainment in the United States. 2013 Census - Detailed Tables. Retrieved from: https://www.census.gov/hhes/socdemo/education/data/cps/2013/tables.html.

USPSTF Program Office. 2013. "U.S. Preventive Services Task Force." U.S. Preventive Services Task Force. http://www.uspreventiveservicestaskforce.org/.

van Manen, M. 1996. *Childhood's Secrets: Intimacy, Privacy, and the Self Reconsidered*. New York: Teacher's College Press.

van Manen, M. 2007. *Researching Lived Experience: Human Science for an Action Sensitive Pedagogy*. Canada: The Althouse Press.

van Zoonen, L. 1994. *Feminist Media Studies*. Thousand Oaks, California: SAGE Publications.

Vardeman, J. E., and L. Aldoory. 2008. "A Qualitative Study of How Women Make Meaning of Contradictory Media Messages About the Risks of Eating Fish." *Health Communication* 23 (3): 282. doi:10.1080/10410230802056396.

Vardeman-Winter, Jennifer. 2012. "Medicalization and Teen Girls' Bodies in the Gardasil Cervical Cancer Vaccine Campaign." *Feminist Media Studies* 12 (2): 281–304. doi:10.1080/14680777.2011.597106.

Vaughan, Peter W., and Everett M. Rogers. 2000. "A Staged Model of Communication Effects: Evidence from an Entertainment-Education Radio Soap Opera in Tanzania." *Journal of Health Communication* 5 (3): 203–27.

Vessey, M., D. Yeates, and S. Flynn. 2010. "Factors Affecting Mortality in a Large Cohort Study with Special Reference to Oral Contraceptive Use." *Contraception* 82 (3): 221–29.

Warren, Samantha, and Joanna Brewis. 2004. "Matter over Mind?" *Sociology* 38 (2): 219–36. doi:10.1177/0038038504040860.

Watkins, Elizabeth Siegel. 2012. "How the Pill Became a Lifestyle Drug: The Pharmaceutical Industry and Birth Control in the United States since 1960." *American Journal Of Public Health* 102 (8): 1462–72. doi:10.2105/AJPH.2012.300706.

Weber, Jutta. 2014. "From Science and Technology to Feminist Technoscience." In *Women, Science, and Technology: A Reader in Feminist Science Studies*, edited by Mary Wyer, Mary Barbercheck, Donna Cookmeyer, Hatice Ozturk, and Marta Wayne, 543–71. New York, NY: Routledge.

Weeks, Brian E., Laura M. Friedenberg, Brian G. Southwell, and Jonathan S. Slater. 2012. "Behavioral Consequences of Conflict-Oriente Health News Coverage: The 2009 Mammography Guideline Controversy and Online Information Seeking." *Health Communication* 27 (2): 158–66.

Wegwarth, O., and G. Gigerenzer. 2011. "'There Is Nothing to Worrry about': Gynecologists' Counseling on Mammography." *Patient Education & Counseling* 84 (2): 251–56.

Welch, H. Gilbert, Lisa M. Schwartz, and Steven Woloshin. 2012. *Overdiagnosed: Making People Sick in the Pursuit of Health*. Boston, MA: Beacon Press.

Whitworth, Melissa, Leanne Bricker, James P. Neilson, and Therese Dowswell. 2010. "Ultrasound for Fetal Assessment in Early Pregnancy." In *Cochrane Database of Systematic Reviews*, edited by The Cochrane Collaboration. Chichester, UK: John Wiley & Sons, Ltd. http://doi.wiley.com/10.1002/14651858.CD007058.pub2.

Wolf, Jacqueline H. 2011. *Deliver Me from Pain: Anesthesia and Birth in America*. Baltimore, MD: The Johns Hopkins University Press.

Wolf, Joan B. 2010. *Is Breast Best?: Taking on the Breastfeeding Experts and the New High Stakes of Motherhood*. NYU Press.

Woloshin, S., L. M. Schwartz, W. C. Black, and B. S. Kramer. 2012. "Cancer Screening Campaigns—Getting Past Uninformative Persuasion." *New England Journal of Medicine* 367 (18): 1677–79. doi:10.1056/NEJMp1209407.

Woo, Jessica G., and Lisa J. Martin. 2015. "Does Breastfeeding Protect Against Childhood Obesity? Moving Beyond Observational Evidence." *Current Obesity Reports*, April, 1–10. doi:10.1007/s13679–015–0148–9.

World Health Organization. 2013. *Family Planning*. 351. http://www.who.int/mediacentre/factsheets/fs351/en/.

———. 2007. "Early Detection." http://www.who.int/cancer/publications/cancer_control_detection/en/index.html.

Wyer, Mary, Mary Barbercheck, Donna Cookmeyer, Hatice Ozturk, and Marta Wayne, eds. 2014. *Women, Science, and Technology: A Reader in Feminist Science Studies*. New York, NY: Routledge.

Zhani, E. E. 2012. "The Joint Commission Expands Performance Measurement Requirements," November 30. http://www.jointcommission.org/the_joint_commission_expands_performance_measurement_requirements/.

Zolna, Mia, and Laura Lindberg. 2012. *Unintended Pregnancy: Incidence and Outcomes Among Young Adult Unmarried Women in the United States, 2001 and 2008*. New York: Guttmacher Institute.http://www.guttmacher.org/pubs/unintended-pregnancy-US-2001-2008 .pdf.

# Index